SWIMMING UPSTREAM

SWIMMING UPSTREAM

THE LITTLE TENNESSEE VALLEY EDUCATIONAL COOPERATIVE

JERRY MORTON

ISBN (EBK): 979-8-9953964-0-6

ISBN (PB): 979-8-9953964-1-3

ISBN (HB): 979-8-9953964-2-0

Publisher: Books by JHM, Knoxville, TN

Cover Design: Sweet Beech Media, Deposit Photos

Swimming Upstream: The Little Tennessee Valley Educational Cooperative— 1st edition (April 2026)

ALSO BY DR. JEROME MORTON

Reluctant Lieutenant: From Basic to OCS in the Sixties (Williams-Ford Texas A&M University Military History Series Book 94)

A School for Healing: Alternative Strategies for Teaching At-Risk Students (with Rosa L. Kennedy)

Finding My Way: A Memoir

This book is dedicated to our master teachers, those children whose joy in experiencing life is not diminished by the limits of their bodies. In turn, it is dedicated to the parents and the many educators who help these bright lights enhance their physical and mental capabilities, enabling the children to better share the love of being.

CONTENTS

FOREWORD

If you are lucky, you will have a particular kind of Friend and Mentor whose lessons you do not fully understand until years—sometimes decades—later. Jerry Morton is that kind of person. I know, because for the past 50 years, I have been that lucky.

In 1975, I was a doctoral student in the School Psychology program at the University of Tennessee—one of the first graduate assistants Jerry recruited to join the Little Tennessee Valley Educational Cooperative (LTVEC), into a group he affectionately called "the cooperative's special ops cadre." He had an eye for people he believed could become effective change agents, and he assembled a remarkable group: diverse in background, rigorous in training, united by a shared dedication to children in need.

After a long work week, every Friday afternoon, that interdisciplinary group gathered at the LTVEC offices under Jerry's leadership. Those meetings were unlike anything I had encountered in my academic training. They were multidisciplinary in the truest sense—a genuine community of practice where we presented cases, wrestled with problems, challenged each other's thinking, and learned to draw on our collective wisdom rather than struggle alone. No one was expected to have all the answers. Jerry made sure of that. And running through every meeting was something equally essential: his humor. Jerry had the rare ability to use laughter not as a distraction from serious work, but as an instrument of it. He taught us, gently but persistently, not to take ourselves too seriously—a lesson that, I have come to understand, is foundational to doing this work well.

I should mention—because Jerry includes it in these pages and remembers it as I do—the day he positioned himself on a high shelf in the storage closet, where he composed himself into the posture of a reclining Buddha, and waited. Patiently. For someone to walk in. That someone was me. And yes, it happened exactly as he describes it. At the time I may have been startled; in retrospect, it was pure Jerry: a moment of playful mischief designed to remind us all that wisdom and levity are not opposites. They are, in fact, partners. And, importantly, it really was funny.

What you hold in your hands is the account of how Jerry Morton built something genuinely rare: an organization tasked with serving children with disabilities across seven school systems in rural East Tennessee, navigating terrain—political, cultural, institutional, and personal—that would have defeated many others. This is not a smooth story. It is a story of resistance and persistence, of crises narrowly averted and coalitions painstakingly built, of bureaucratic walls scaled and, occasionally, walked around. Jerry navigated all of it, and this book tells you how.

What makes this book exceptional, however, is not merely the story itself but the way Jerry tells it. He is a natural storyteller, and he understands instinctively what the best teachers have always known: you must show before you tell. Each episode in these pages is rendered with enough vivid detail that you feel the stakes, sense the resistance, and grasp the dilemma—and only then does Jerry draw back the curtain to name the principle at work.

Consider one of the most deceptively simple formulations in the book: "Your words have to be congruent with what you mean when you say something. Your behavior has to be congruent with what you say. If you ask a teacher to be eighty percent positive in her corrective instructions to a student, you have to be eighty percent positive in your coaching of her as she implements new educational and behavioral strategies." This is not a complicated idea. But it is a demanding one, and Jerry's narrative earns it. You see it fail, and you see it work. By the time he states it plainly, it has already become self-evident.

Equally powerful is his discussion of what he calls the trap of the "hero." The change agent who positions themselves as the indispensable leader—the one whose vision and drive make everything possible—is, paradoxically, failing at the core task. As Jerry explains, "Being the 'hero' means that those you have assisted have become dependent upon your leading them to their successes. When the hero of the story leaves the community, the community cannot maintain that success. They have lost their leader." The goal, Jerry insists, is not to be needed. The goal is to leave behind a community that no longer needs you.

This is the architecture of the book: narrative, then principle; story, then template. Jerry has embedded his framework inside his memoir with considerable craft, trusting readers to extract the lessons as they emerge. But he is also generous enough, at key moments, to state those lessons explicitly—to ensure that the wisdom embedded in the experience does not get lost in the telling.

I did not fully understand, when I joined the Little Tennessee Valley Educational Cooperative as a young doctoral student, what I was being taught. I understood the techniques. I absorbed the frameworks. But the deeper lesson—that the work of a change agent is ultimately the work of building capacity in others, of sharpening your consulting skills so finely that you become, in the end, unnecessary—that took years to fully land. I carried those teachings with me into hospital and medical settings across the rest of my career, and I found them as applicable there as they had been in the schools of East Tennessee. The contexts changed. The principles held.

You are fortunate. You do not have to wait for the lessons to arrive slowly, the way they came to me. Jerry Morton has put them on the page for you. You have the benefit of his wisdom, his stories, and his hard-won experience—distilled and made accessible in ways that my generation had to absorb through many Friday afternoon meetings and the occasional encounter with a reclining Buddha on a high shelf.

Read carefully. Follow the templates he has placed within the narrative. Leave behind a community that no longer needs you. And do not, under any circumstances, take yourself too seriously.

~ Barry Nierenberg, PhD, ABPP
Board Certified in Rehabilitation Psychology
March 2026

PREFACE

My goal in sharing the early history of the educational cooperative is to help those involved as facilitators of change to understand better some of the difficulties they may encounter. That understanding could be translated into the development of helpful strategies. When you enter a situation in which you have to introduce major change in the behavior of others, there will be resistance. The source of that resistance comes from the belief systems of those you are trying to assist. For example, before being employed by the Little Tennessee Valley Educational Cooperative (an organization of seven school system sharing service providers), I had the job of being the first regularly scheduled school psychologist to deliver services to seven all-black elementary schools being integrated for the first time. In one elementary school, the black principal refused to meet with me. When we finally did meet, he told me that I had to be the worst school psychologist the school system had. The system would only send white staff to black schools that the system did not want to work with white children or staff. I did not need to show up on my assigned days to his school. He did not want me there. I said that I could not do that, that I would respond to any teacher's request for assistance with a child. Later in the school year, we learned to respect each other. He was supportive of my work. Among the things he confided to me was the reason he was so stern with the children and frequently paddled them for minor offenses. He said that the white culture in his city was so cruel to black people that he had to harden the children to that cruelty. This hardening would enable them to survive as adults.

The belief systems in all of us are difficult to change because we find ways to reinforce them constantly. Those we select as friends reflect our core values. The churches we attend, the social gatherings we participate in all agree with what we believe to be true. After all, I am a good person; so are you and so are our friends. How could good people do anything but what is right and just? Our tendency is to ignore or reinterpret any behavior in our friends that does not fit our concept of being a good person.

The people charged with bringing change into a system have their own belief systems and locked-in behaviors that sometimes hinder the change process but can also be a significant asset. It is important to recognize that the people who are resisting the change are good people. They think they are right and you are wrong. Sometimes they are correct. You are the one making the mistake. Learning the way the person resisting the change interprets their view of the situation often provides insights for strategies to enable them to adopt your point of view.

I have interwoven two perspectives into the historical narrative of those early years. I share with the reader my memory of events as they happened. Naturally, those memories may have become clouded with the passage of time. As time passed, I learned more about the circumstances of the events I recalled. Those greater understandings are also reflected in many parts of the narrative.

This journey allowed me acquainted me with many, many talented and gifted educators dedicated to assisting children and with some personalities that had a greater focus on other goals. We all learned. We all made progress. In some cases, it took years for the resisters to realize the value of the changes we were championing, but they took place. That is the important part of this story. The vision of the educational cooperative has remained alive.

Within the manuscript, I provide the reader with an account of the belief systems I brought into my role as the person directing the development of new and extensive services for children with disabilities within the public-school systems the cooperative served. I will share encountering belief systems within those schools that sometimes supported my beliefs and sometimes resisted them. In turn, the narrative will reflect how some of the beliefs held by individuals within the systems changed and some remained the same. The major change I encountered in my understandings was a greater realization of the time it takes for some core beliefs to change within the wider culture.

~JM

ONE
THE CONCEPT OF THE THE LITTLE TENNESSEE EDUCATIONAL COOPERATIVE

It was during my employment interview with the cooperative's Executive Director, Bill Oakes, that I first learned about the Little Tennessee Valley Educational Cooperative (LTVEC), an organization of seven school systems. If I remember correctly, that was around April of 1973. I was preparing for my defense of my doctoral dissertation for the Ph. D. degree in psychology from the University of Tennessee (UT) at Knoxville. My specialty area in psychology was school psychology. The psychology department had just started offering a doctorate in school psychology two years earlier. I was one of fifteen or so students who were in the first group admitted to that specialty area and would be the first of that group to graduate from the program. My past experiences in the area of psychology had provided me with knowledge that allowed me to progress rapidly through the department's mandatory levels of achievement, which had to be completed before I was allowed to form a doctoral committee and begin my dissertation research project.

My past experiences in psychological issues were key factors in the strategies used by LTVEC during its formative years. A knowledge of those strategies is helpful in understanding LTVEC's role in creating the delivery model for school psychological and special education services within the co-op's seven school systems while also aiding in implementing the state's new special education law. I had received a master's degree in school psychology from Miami University of Ohio in August 1966. I was scheduled to do a year's internship in Ohio's Hamilton County School System for the 1966-1967 school year. The internship was required in order to become certified as a school psychologist in Ohio.

A few days after completing the degree requirements, I was compelled by the country's military draft system to join the Army. My year of Army training included basic training, advanced infantry training and infantry officer school, OCS. Upon completion of OCS, I was commissioned as a second lieutenant in the infantry. I was to receive two weeks' leave before attending airborne school, psychological warfare school and then to receive further orders. Within days of my OCS graduation date, my orders were changed. All previous orders were canceled. I was to report immediately to the commanding officer of the Army's Special Warfare Center at Fort Bragg, North Carolina.

Upon arriving at Fort Bragg, I learned that I was to develop the psychology classes for a staff officer's course in psychological warfare just being created, as well as to develop other areas of instruction and then to be the instructor for those classes. I was replacing a retiring lieutenant. colonel. He was an excellent mentor as I had no meaningful understanding of the military's concept of psychological warfare. From the colonel I learned that the focus of psychological operations, PSYOPS, was to understand the values and mores of people living in other cultures and then to prepare military officers to be effective communicators with them. My training in school psychology, as well as other life experiences, had taught me the importance of quickly learning the mores and customs of people I did not know but had to interact with. I knew that everyone wants to be valued and respected. The importance of finding ways to communicate your positive regard of someone within their cultural context is important. This is particularly true when promoting the development of new behaviors. Assisting a classroom teacher to develop new strategies for teaching a child better ways of doing things requires the same cultural and situational awareness needed to assist a military officer involved in engaging the support of rural villagers from another country.

The colonel emphasized that it was always important to tell the truth. Lies would always be discovered. When that occurred, all the truthful messages would be discredited as if they were lies as well. The Colonel humorously repeated to me in emphasizing the importance of clarity in your communications to others a quotation from Lewis Carroll's *Alice in Wonderland.* The Mad Hatter reportedly says "Don't do what I say. Do what I mean when I say it."

The colonel also felt that it was important to explain John F. Kennedy's intent in creating the Special Warfare Center. Its mission was to train Special Forces and related military personnel to be teachers to the citizens of other countries our nation was assisting in insurgent/counter-insurgent warfare activities. As I stated earlier, my training in school psychology had taught me the importance of valuing others and understanding their points of view, as well as the use of positive reinforcement in the role of assisting educators to develop programs for children with special needs. During my two years at the Special Warfare Center, I was able to develop instructional materials supporting these concepts. The Army saw to it that I had access to multiple sources of information, including state-of-the-art academic research on cross-cultural issues.

As a result of my studies in the Army and my interactions with the professional Special Warfare officers, my concepts of the role of a change agent came into clearer perspective. When you are teaching others new behaviors of any kind, you are being an agent of change. Your goal is for the learner to be able to implement the new way of doing something without your being present. If the learner can accomplish the new behavior only in the presence of the teacher, then the educator has failed. Success is demonstrated by the independent implementation of the lessons learned. That is the reward.

Having been discharged from the Army, I became employed in August 1969, by the Florida Pinellas County School System as a school psychologist. I was assigned to be the school psychologist serving seven inner-city schools of St. Petersburg, Florida. The school system was being integrated for the first time. The first year of my employment, the school system was having white teachers and school staff begin working in the formerly all-black schools while sending some black educators to work in the all-white schools. The second year of my employment the system began sending some white children into the formerly all-black schools and black children into the formerly all-white schools. I considered my work at the Special Warfare Center to have been excellent training for this role.

During my two years in the St. Petersburg schools, I developed a positive reinforcement system for the teachers to implement in managing classroom behavior. The first teacher I worked with and then TV taped, to use in training others, was an extremely gifted and brave black woman. I wish I could explain to you how talented she was. She opened my eyes to the many dedicated and gifted black educators who had devoted their lives to helping children in need. This teacher's husband was equally as gifted in his role as a guidance counselor at my junior high school.

Then there were the outstanding black school principals. The school system's administrative staff was committed to providing all of us with superior training in new strategies, often engaging outside experts. I learned from the University of Florida's Charles Madsen, Jr. the positive reinforcement system he had developed. The school system sent several of us to learn encounter group strategies at training sites throughout the country during the summer of 1970. I attended the training program in Portland, Oregon. Dr. Vi. Brody graciously taught me her developmental play therapeutic strategy in assisting young children with behavior difficulties during my second year in the system. I was able to conduct many in-services for educators both within the system and across Florida at various professional conferences.

Some of the important things I learned from that experience included realizing the incredible talent and dedication of so many teachers from both races, realizing that a high percentage of children have various conditions that hinder their learning process, and observing the lack of adequate resources to meaningfully address those needs despite the fact that there were and are proven strategies that could be applied. Another realization I gained was the role that fear played within some individuals when they are confronted with change. Often, when individuals find themselves in a hard to manage situation, they see a great deal of risk in trying to implement a new strategy. If it doesn't work, their situation will be much worse. This fear has to be overcome, not through the use of intimidation and force, but through positive support and coaching that is long lasting.

It is not enough for someone to present a two-hour workshop on a new strategy that took that professional many years to learn and then walk away expecting the attendees to implement that strategy perfectly. It is important for the expert's behavior to reflect the principles being taught. The expert also needs to cause adequate support to be provided to the teacher if the successful adaptation of the new strategy is to be achieved. The teacher has to be able to implement the strategy long after the expert is gone. If this does not happen, the failure of implementation becomes the proof that the new way of doing things does not work. Once created, that negative belief system is hard to overcome. My experiences had taught me that it is best to be as successful as possible during the first phase of developing new behaviors in others.

After the end of my two years in the schools, I became a doctoral student in the psychology department at the University of Tennessee. My first year in the program was the department's first full year of the specialty area in school psychology. Our entering group of fifteen or so was a group of carefully selected students who were as talented as they were dedicated to helping children and working with school system staff in passing on their knowledge.

In addition to their course work, every graduate student in the psychology department was required to work twenty hours per week with some organization involved in public service. For me and my group, it had to be with an organization serving children. It did not matter if you were receiving payment as a graduate assistant or not. During my first year, I worked at a nonprofit center that assisted both troubled children and their parents. I worked with the parents there in establishing positive reinforcement programs and in developmental play strategies. The director of that program and I became lifelong friends over the course of our professional lives. I served as an intern school psychologist as a paid graduate assistant during my second year at UT in the Knoxville City School System. Since I met the state's requirement as a fully functioning school psychologist at that time. That's how the system utilized my services during the twenty hours of work per week over the course of the school year.

During that time, I also served as a consultant to the school system's integration project to enhance that program's efforts. Again, life-long friendships were established with many of the professionals in that system. As you would expect, I shared many of my experiences as a master's level school psychologist in the schools being integrated for the first time with my fellow students. We seemed to share the same core philosophies concerning the valuing of others and the use of positive reinforcement in our role as change agents.

It was through my activities with the Knoxville School System that Dr. Bill Oakes learned that I was about to graduate and was looking for a position as a doctoral-level school psychologist for the 1973-1974 school year. His call came to my home one spring evening. After identifying himself, he explained that the cooperative was looking for a doctoral level school psychologist to set up a school psychology delivery system for its seven-member school systems and to assist the systems to meet the requirements of the state's new special education law. Implementation of the law was to begin for the first time in the 1973-1974 school year. The state's plan for this first year had the school systems identify the disabled children in their school districts whose disabilities were interfering with their ability to benefit from the regular education program.

Once those children had been identified and plans made to implement more appropriate educational strategies for each child, the system would fully implement those strategies during the second year, the 1974-1975 school year. For the 1973-1974 school year, the state was providing every school system one dollar per child for the evaluation of children to determine who had a disability and if that disability met the law's requirements for determining that there was a need to adjust the child's regular educational program for progress to take place. Naturally, the changes needed to be identified, and periodic evaluations made to verify the planned improvements. This enabled the seven school systems to provide the cooperative with one hundred thousand dollars to hire school psychologists for accomplishing the mission. Dr. Oakes said I had been highly recommended to him by a senior supervisor in the city's school system. He thought I would be a good candidate for creating such a system. We agreed upon an interview date and location.

During the interview Bill explained the history of the creation of the cooperative and its mission. LTVEC was created to manage the human services component of new model city that was to be built by the Tennessee Valley Authority with the completion of the Little Tennessee River dam project. At that moment, the completion of the dam was on hold due to a lawsuit filed against TVA upon the discovery of the snail darter, a small fish that had just been discovered living in the Little Tennessee River. The suit claimed that the river was its only known habitat. Creating a lake out of the river would destroy the habitat of the snail darter. Biologists were currently trying to discover if the snail darter lived in other similar waterways.

Once the suit was settled in TVA's favor, the model city project,

Timberlake, would resume in force. The center of the city would be in the area of Vonore, Tennessee. That was the location of the center of the lake, Tellico Lake, the lake that would be created by closing the dam. Lenoir City, the nearest relatively large metropolitan area, was about fifteen miles southwest of Vonore. The dam would empty water into the Tennessee River just below the Loudon Lake Dam at Lenoir City. Tellico Lake water would be joined with the Loudon Lake. The two lakes would meet just above the newly built dam.

The Vonore area was selected as the center of Timberlake because that was where the three counties most impacted, Blount, Loudon and Monroe, came together. The plan called for the model city to be an exemplar of a planned community. The water of the lake would be so clean around the model city that one could take a boat to the center of the lake, dip in a glass for water and drink it without risk of illness. All the utilities of the city would be underground. There would be a mix of economically diverse populations living in it. Stores, community centers, entertainment centers, schools, etc., would all be in walking distance. There was to be little need for cars to drive in the area. Just a little way to the southwest of the city and Vonore would be an industrial center. Vonore and the area of the industrial center were in Monroe County. Many of the Timberlake residents would work there.

A little to the northwest of the model city and Vonore, in Loudon County along the shores of the lake, would be residential housing developments. To the east of Vonore was Blount County and the beginning of the Smoky Mountains. That area would be designated for vacation homes, recreational water activities and outdoor adventures.

Legislation was being prepared to provide for the sharing of the tax base across the three counties in the Timberlake area. Since Monroe County would be the industrial center of the project, it would generate the largest tax revenue. Loudon County would have a large influx of new residents in the planned housing areas, and it would need extra tax dollars to service those residents. In turn,

Blount County would have a large increase in recreational activities that would need new tax dollars. The sharing of the revenue generated by the development of industry in Monroe County would accommodate the new financial demands created by the Timberlake project in the other two counties.

Bill and I met several times before I was to be interviewed by the cooperative's board of directors. During those meetings, I learned a lot about him. His quick understanding of my role at the Special Warfare Center prompted me to ask about his military experiences. He had been a career Army officer in its specialized ranger units before earning a doctorate in English, teaching at the University of Tennessee and becoming the administrative assistant to the president of the Tennessee University System. Through his role with the university system, Bill had interacted with many legislators, government officials, labor leaders, TVA and various national organizations. He had been able to facilitate the passage of legislation that allowed the cooperative to become an extension of the school systems with the cooperative's staff having all of the rights and benefits of any educator working for a public school system. For reasons I did not understand, the cooperative staff was not able to become a part of the teacher retirement system until the 1974-1975 school year.

Bill provided me with a copy of the special education laws. I needed to learn them by the time of my interview with the board of directors in early June. There would be many questions about it and the role of the school psychological services program. He also expected the board to inquire as to how the school psychological and special education services would be set up so that every system received their fair share of those services. For planning purposes, we were to assume that the seven systems would provide the cooperative with approximately $100,000. The basic plan was to hire me as the director of the services. I would recruit advanced graduate students from the UT Psychology Department specializing in school psychology. At that time the current payment for these graduate students was $4,000 and mileage for their travel from the cooperative's central office in Alcoa to their assigned schools and back. That was for twenty hours of service per week. We would also have to budget for the additional costs of Social Security payments, retirement, etc. that all employers had to pay the government. A full-time trainer of educators would also be employed to conduct workshops on the new laws. That person's reimbursement would be established once we determined the actual amount of funding to be provided. I would also be providing training sessions on the laws to the school systems.

My primary role with the graduate assistants was to supervise their activities, ensure the accuracy of their work, provide professional backup support in unusual or difficult cases they might encounter, and conduct training sessions to school system personnel in positive reinforcement strategies and developmental play sessions for children with behavioral difficulties. I would also be involved in testing and evaluating the more complex cases that might arise across system boundaries. The cooperative and I were responsible for the delivery of professional psychological services to the school systems. The demands of that responsibility would make it difficult to monitor the presence of professional staff's attendance within the schools on a daily basis. Therefore, the school systems would be responsible for monitoring staff members' attendance at a particular school at the scheduled time. If a staff member was not in attendance at the prearranged time, the school system was to notify the cooperative's central office and the problem would be corrected.

The school psychology interns were to be assigned to specific school systems. They were to consider that school system to be theirs. If that system decided to terminate school psych services, then the cooperative would work to make up the lost time with other school systems. However, all the interns were assured that they would not be out of a job with their school system simply because another intern had been with the cooperative for a longer period of time. In essence, an intern held tenure for serving in the assigned school system as long as funding for the position was available and work performance met professional standards.

The school systems were concerned that the money they paid the cooperative for psych and other services would be spent for services to other school systems. To ensure that each system received its fair share of services, the percentage of the total funds provided for the services through the cooperative would be reflected in a monthly report to the board of directors. If a system's share of the total $100,000 provided was $10,000, then it should have ten percent of the total number of children given full psycho-educational testing that month, ten percent of the teacher conferences held, ten percent of the parent conferences held, ten percent of staff training events, etc.

A list of approximately twelve specific school psychological activities performed by the staff was developed. All of these activities would be reported in total and by school system monthly. Any discrepancies in those reports would be explained by me and any necessary adjustments would be initiated. This would be and was a tedious task, but it was necessary to prove to the systems that each one was being treated fairly. No school system would be exploiting the others through the cooperative.

Another concern of the systems was that the cooperative would spend too much of their funds on administrative costs. Therefore, they wanted a monthly accounting of those costs. They wanted the funds provided to be focused on services rather than on unreasonably high administrative expenses.

TWO

THE QUICK HISTORY OF THE LITTLE TENNESSEE VALLEY EDUCATIONAL COOPERATIVE NOW KNOWN AS THE TENNESSEE EDUCATIONAL COOPERATIVE

This quick review of the creation and development of the Little Tennessee Valley Educational Cooperative, LTVEC, simply touches key factual information. The Tennessee Valley Authority, TVA, around 1965 decided to dam the Little Tennessee River and create a model city. TVA's goal was to demonstrate to the country how economic and social development would be enhanced in the East Tennessee Region by damming the river and owning large areas of land surrounding the lake that would be created through the damming.

By controlling a large amount of land around the new lake, TVA could facilitate the large economic impact the lake would produce. It was reasoned that the lack of predicted economic development around other TVA-created lakes was due to TVA's not being able to control what happened to the surrounding land. TVA contracted with the University of Tennessee at Knoxville to create recommendations for the best strategies to follow in achieving TVA's goals.

The study was called a Charrette. The Charrette's members included university experts and members of the communities to be affected by the project. One of the recommendations of the study was the creation of an educational cooperative to develop and manage both the school system of the model city and the human services that would be needed by the city's residents as well to provide enhanced services to the surrounding area. The educational cooperative's board of directors was to be an elected official from each of the surrounding communities and a school board member from the impacted area schools.

Since the center of the lake, Tellico Lake, was at Vonore, Tennessee, TVA had decided that would also be where the model city would be built and that the surrounding lake area would contain the economic, housing and recreational development that would take place. Blount, Loudon and Monroe Counties came together within the immediate area of Vonore. Therefore, the three county school systems and the four city school systems located in those counties became members of the cooperative as did an elected official from each of the three county governments. A county commissioner from each county and a school board member from each of the seven school systems became the members of LTVEC's Board of Directors. This group decided to include the school superintendents from its school systems in LTVEC's Board of Directors. The board began to have monthly meetings in the evenings in a basement room of a local bank's branch building near the center of the projected model city at Vonore.

The initial funding for the creation of the model city and the educational cooperative was to come from TVA and the federal government. Federal programs, such as HUD, would be the major funding source for the model city. TVA would be the key funding source for the beginning stages of the cooperative. Those funds would be used primarily as startup administrative costs. The industrial development was planned to take place in Monroe County near Vonore. Housing development needed outside the boundaries of the model city would be in Loudon County with secondary homes and recreational development in Blount County. The primary tax base would be in Monroe County with its industrial development. Using that tax revenue for projects in the other two counties would require approval from the Tennessee legislators. TVA was confident that the state's legislators would approve that revenue sharing.

Dr. Bill Oakes was employed as the executive director of LTVEC in August 1971. Dr. Oakes employed Ms. Glynden Calhoun to be LTVEC's bookkeeper/secretary shortly after his appointment. LTVEC's administrative offices were located in Vonore, Tennessee. I was told that a fire at that location in early 1973 caused the loss of many of the records Dr. Oakes had accumulated that documented many of the early activities in the creation of LTVEC. The fire forced LTVEC to relocate its central offices to the administrative building of Alcoa City Schools. The school system generously donated several former classrooms in their administrative building for LTVEC's use.

At the time Jerry Morton was employed by LTVEC in July 1973, the member school systems were paying an annual fee to cover the basic administrative costs of the cooperative. Those costs included salaries for Dr. Oakes and Ms. Calhoun and other expenses such as office supplies, communications costs and travel reimbursements. After the total annual administrative cost was determined, each school system was billed a percentage of the cost as determined by the school system's percentage of its student population to the total student population of all of the member school systems.

The cooperative membership contract stipulated that if a school system decided that it wanted to withdraw from being a member of the cooperative, it must give the cooperative a full school year's notice. During that year of notice to withdraw, the school system had to continue to pay its membership fee. This meant that if a system gave notice of withdrawal in March of 1976 it would remain a member of the cooperative until the completion of the next full school year, July 1976, to the end of June 1977. In the event of the complete closure of the cooperative, the contract stated that the member school systems at the time of closure would divide the assets of the cooperative on the basis of each system's school population as compared to the current total.

Jerry Morton, soon to receive his Ph.D., was employed as the director of psychological and special education services to create a delivery model for school psychological services to the seven school systems and to assist the school systems to develop special education services that met the requirements of the special education laws passed by the state of Tennessee in 1972 and by Congress in 1973. The seven-member school systems used the specialized funding provided them by the state's department of education for the purpose of creating a system to determine which students qualified for special education services and to begin the process of providing the needed services. The systems were allocated one dollar per child based on their student populations. In turn, the systems provided LTVEC with a total of $100,000.00 to create a psychological assessment process of their students. Each system received the percentage of services provided by the cooperative on the basis of the percentage of the total funds provided for this service. Blount County Schools provided forty percent of the $100,000.00, so it received forty percent of the service.

In December 1975, Dr. Oakes had an accidental death. Dr. Morton became the cooperative's executive director in addition to his other duties and remained in that position until his retirement. Dr. Morton retired in 2014 but continued as a part-time employee of the cooperative in the role of coordinator of the Tennessee Internship Consortium in Psychology for the 2014-2015 school year while also volunteering his time to continue being the executive director of the cooperative. After that school year, for a short period of time, one and then another person served as the executive director of LTVEC. They had not been previously employed by the co-op and had difficulty grasping its complexities. From 2016 to 2022 Pam Potocik served as the co-op's executive director while continuing in her role as the coordinator of LTVEC's Birth-to-Three program. Jana Hackworth, coordinator of LTVEC's Extended School Program, became LTVEC's executive director in 2022 and continues in that role as of this writing.

The Extended School Program began as one after-school enrichment program and grew to provide many after-school and before-school activities designed to enrich and enhance students' educational experience. Throughout the years since Dr. Morton's tenure with the cooperative, Stephenie Glass, bookkeeper/office manager, provided the knowledge base that gave reassuring stability as the baton of leadership passed from person to person. By 2024, LTVEC was delivering such a wide variety of services to multiple school systems in the state that the cooperative changed its name to better reflect its role in delivering services to school systems in Tennessee. The Little Tennessee Valley Educational Cooperative's name was changed to the Tennessee Educational Cooperative (TEC). To learn more about the multiple services of the Tennessee Educational Cooperative, visit its website, www.tn-edu.org.

THREE
AN OUTSIDER'S LOOK AT THE BEGINNING YEARS

In July 1973, Jerry Morton was employed by LTVEC to create school psychological and special education services. His knowledge of the creation of the cooperative prior to that time was limited. His focus on the tasks before him left little time to explore the cooperative's creation. Fortunately, a three-year grant from the U.S. Department of Education's Office of Environmental Education that began in 1977 had contracted with the University of Illinois to conduct a qualitative evaluation of LTVEC's program. The study, conducted by Dr. Robert Stake and Ph.D. candidate Claire Brown, began in the spring of 1979 and was published in August 1979. It begins with a review of the creation of LTVEC prior to July 1973. LTVEC was one of two programs evaluated in the report, titled "Evaluating A Regional Environmental Learning System."

The section of the study for LTVEC titled "Beginnings," starts on page 12 and concludes on page 28:

PG. 12:

<u>Dee's Cafe, Loudon City</u>

Nanny, you ready to pay or you just gettin' a paper?

Nanny opens her handbag.
Ain't nothing in here.
How much is it?

A dollar.

Nanny pays in change.

Nanny, you been to a doctor?

No, doctors can't do nothin' for me.

Sometimes.
Could give you something for that cold.

That's what's got me messed up now.
Takin' too much medicine.
Give me one of them plastic bags.
Ain't no use wastin' this
good piece of meat.

You need somethin' that will knock it out of you.
I'll take you, if you'll go.
Which doctor do you go to?

I'll go to most any of them.
Have I paid you?

Yeah, you done paid us, Nanny.
    If you want to go to the doctor...

PG.13:

Coming to know the Little Tennessee Valley Co-operative is more than an intellectual probe of an educational program. It's a knowing of context that seeps through your pores, beginning from the moment the Delta 727 settles down at the airport, halfway between Knoxville and Maryville (pronounced Murvul), and a southern drawl beside you says, "Yeah, feels like we're back on good ole Tennessee dirt."

I'm not sure what hearing Rocky Top blasting from jukeboxes and pick-'em-up trucks, hoping Nanny gets to a doctor, watching the deer graze in Cade's Cove or redbirds play about in the brush beside the Little Tennessee have to do with LIVE; but somehow, for this observer, they all became one. These experiences were much a part of a growing attunement to the woven consistency of people, land, and rivers; where change is so slow as to be almost imperceptible; where the passing of springtime is charted in morning hoar frosts on the mountains, and the coming of dogwood winter; and where environmental education is sometimes teaching kids how to clean fish.

PG. 14:

THE SEVEN SCHOOL DISTRICTS

The Little Tennessee Valley Educational Cooperative has, from the start, been made up of seven participating school districts--the three county districts of the Little Tennessee Valley--Loudon, Blount, and Monroe--as well as four city systems within those counties--Lenoir City, Sweet-water, Maryville, and Alcoa. Altogether, there are approximately 29,000 public school children in the seven-county area and within the LTVEC region.

By regions, the size of the districts, according to student population, varies as follows:

Blount County 11,000
Monroe County 4,000
Loudon County. 3,000
Maryville City 2,500
Lenoir City 2,500
Alcoa City 1,300
Sweetwater City. 1,300

There are several distinctions between the county and the city systems. The three county systems are larger, more rural and administrated by elected superintendents, whereas the smaller city systems are administered by superintendents appointed by their school boards.

In addition, each district has a distinct personality with significant geographic, economic, and cultural distinctions. The scope of this study did not include in-depth inquiry into each school district.As observations were being conducted through the districts, however, a few quotations and vignettes which tell something of the character of the districts were saved, and are simply shared below in the form in which they came to the observer:

Blount County

Blount is one of the oldest counties in Tennessee, having been developed and given official status by the Tennessee Territorial Legislature on July 11, 1795. The territory forming the new county had originally been part of Knox County. A county court for the new county was organized in September, 1795. Blount County

Blount County was named for William Blount, Governor of the Southwest Territory. Maryville, the county seat, was named in honor of Governor Blount's wife, Mary Grainger Blount.

PG. 15:

The settlement of the Blount County area got underway in a substantial way around 1785, when there was a heavy immigration from North Carolina and Virginia. There were some scattered settlers prior to 1785. Apparently, the earliest white settlers had much trouble with Indian raiders.

"Blount County is wealthy, but has a low tax rate. Its financial base is Alcoa Aluminum and Knoxville. It has a very low property tax. People who commute to Knoxville don't care about the political scene in Blount County. Landed farmers have the political power. But they are extremely conservative and don't want to pay *taxes. People in Blount County who are well-educated are demanding better services, but the county can't afford them. Blount County is eighth or ninth in wealth in the state and eighteenth in taxes collected."*

"Local governments aren't going to raise taxes for facilities."

"Consolidation is one of our big issues."

Loudon County

Loudon County became a legal entity on May 21, 1870, and [as] Christiana County.

The name was changed a few days later to Loudon County. The county, formed from parts of Blount, Monroe, and Roane Counties, was named in commemoration of Fort Loudon, Colonial British fort near where the Tellico River flows into the Little Tennessee River near Niles Ferry Bridge on Highway 411. The fort itself was named for the Earl of Loudon, Commander-in-Chief of the British Forces in America and also Governor of Virginia. The fort was erected in 1756; it is supposed to have been the first structure of its kind created in Tennessee by Anglo-Americans. The fort was destroyed by the Cherokee Indians in 1760.

The first church in the county was built by the Rev. Isaac

Anderson, a teacher of Sam Houston and founder of Maryville College. The date was 1823.

"In our district there were problems around the mid 170s—the handicapped law and trying to comply. . . .Now it's not our major problem. In fact, I can't think of any major problem now."

PG. 16:

<u>Monroe County</u>

Monroe County became a legal entity in 1819, having been developed from lands obtained by the Hiwassee Purchase made by the Federal Government from the Cherokee Indians. The county was named for the fifth President of the United States, James Monroe (1817-1825), a native of Virginia.

The present county seat was named for President James Madison, the fourth President (1809-1817), also a native of Virginia. The site for Madisonville was probably selected in 1822, but the town was not plotted until 1827. Apparently the first and second county courts were held at Morganton (now in Loudon County) and at Henderson, east of Madisonville. The territory, now in Monroe County, contains the territory occupied by the Cherokee Indian towns of Chota, Tellico, Citico and Toqua. The earliest permanent settlers came largely from Virginia, South Carolina and North Carolina.

"We're basically slow to change. The longer I live, the more I see merit to this."

"Of the seven Co-op districts, Monroe County has the lowest per capita income. The tax base is strictly property. It's an agricultural-based county. Our biggest challenge is getting people to accept responsibility of where they are education wise. Many of our children have not had the cultural advantages of things in the home, etc."

"Our people are a mixture of Appalachian Mountain people, and small town people. The mountain people are slow to accept, defensive, and hold back. They are slow for change and very cautious."

Lenoir City

"Most people work in Lenoir City, in Oakridge, Knoxville, or for TVA. This is the place where they sleep at night. Twenty-five percent of the kids' parents are federally connected. I feel we are in the process of change—industrial development in the city and county, a change process, so that the biggest concern now is providing for

PG. 17:

living in this area. There is an increase of kids in the schools. If Expo '80 comes to Knoxville, and if the Tellico Project ever gets out of the county and gets development going . . . But we had better do some planning. We could not accommodate it."

"We feel we never did leave the basics to go back to. We never did go to the new math. We're still somewhat traditional, and if that is not good, I guess we feel that is tried and proved."

ALCOA

"We have a significant number of black kids--twenty-eight to thirty percent. We have the best tax base in the state--from all the plants of the Aluminum Company of America (ALCOA) that are here."

"We've got all we need: we're the richest school system in the state."

"Population is a problem--declining enrollment. Alcoa retirees are buying up the houses. It's difficult to maintain quality."

Sweetwater

"There was a settler who came out and built a house on the hill above the spring. In this house, the man had a large molasses barrel. This was originally the home of the Cherokee Indians. One day some Cherokees came down through the Cherokee forest, got drunk, and they went up and set the man's house on fire. The molasses barrel tumbled into the creek, and the Cherokees named the spot 'Spring of Sweet Water.'"

"The people here are of Scotch-Irish descent—hardworking, energetic, outgoing, have done a lot of things for themselves."

"Basics are our main concern, meeting standards. We are a traditional school, textbook-oriented. We're trying to eliminate things from the outside that might distract from the basics."

PG. 18:

BEGINNINGS

The history of the Little Tennessee Valley Cooperative is not a single story, but several, each a view from a different window. Joe Sherlan, superintendent of Sweetwater City Schools, was there and remembers the beginnings this way:

TVA, in planning for Tellico, decided they needed grassroot support. And if Tellico came to fruition they would need educational support. . . .They would have to cross county lines because the project was across three counties. So out of this came the Charrette . . . and then the Cooperative (LTVEC).

A report by a study group from the University of Tennessee describing the activities of the Little Tennessee Valley Charette also described the Cooperative's beginnings:

For about four years the Tellico Area Planning Council has been developing plans for the proposed "Timberlake" community to encompass parts of three counties, Blount, Loudon, and Monroe. As one aspect of this process, the seven superintendents in the area formed a committee to consider the educational dimensions of the projected community. During their discussions it became apparent that it was inadequate to consider educational planning just for the Timberlake community. It was decided that educational planning should include the entire three county area.

A group representing the seven public school systems and the local governments in the Blount, Loudon, and Monroe tri-county area, therefore, instigated the development of a series of meetings designed to gain widespread community involvement in education. The "charrette" technique was selected in order to facilitate multi-group involvement in the geographical area and to provide a means for studying and resolving educational problems within the context of total community needs.

"It is proposed that the school systems involved in the Little Tennessee Valley Charrette form a confederation of local school districts to be called the "Little Tennessee Valley Educational Cooperative.

PG. 19:

"It is further proposed that this educational cooperative be formed under the General Act of the General Assembly of the State of Tennessee known as the "Educational Cooperation Act," Public Chapter No. 511. This act permits "Boards of Education the most efficient use of their powers by enabling them to cooperate with other localities on a basis of mutual advantage and to thereby provide educational services and facilities in a manner that will accord best with geographic, economic, population, and other factors influencing the needs and the development of local educational facilities and services."

As part of its planning toward the Tellico Dam Project, to be implemented in the Little Tennessee River Valley, TVA stimulated the concurrent planning of the model city, Timberlake. To parallel these activities, TVA was further instrumental in the organization of the Tellico Area Planning Council and the eventual organization of the Little Tennessee Valley Educational Cooperative. The organization of the Co-op was undoubtedly seen as an advantage by TVA. Support of the project and cooperative planning among local school people for the future of Timberlake could be a foothold in gaining more general support of local people for the Tellico Project. Thus LTVEC was created, in one sense, a forced marriage among geographically linked but historically independent school districts. Why would TVA work through the educational systems in gaining political support? Because in the Little Tennessee Valley, schools were not only central to community life and community interest; but also significant in community political activity. Or, as one person interviewed put it:

Education in the South is like motherhood and apple pie. It's looked upon as being sacred . . .They can wave the flag more for education than for anything.

For the local districts, the Cooperative was certainly not a pro-active, spontaneous coalition of seven school districts committed to cooperative educational activities.

LTVEC was instead a local shared reaction, probably more political and economic than educational, in response to the external press of a special environmental circumstance; i.e., Timberlake. These earliest participants in the Charrette recognized the wisdom of unity in the face of the coming of Timberlake, an intruder at once dazzling and ominous.

Stakes were high. The location of control of the educational system of Timberlake would be a critical problem of the community itself and to surrounding counties.

PG. 20:

It is imperative that the three counties cooperate regarding the Timberlake project. Should the project be developed as proposed, Loudon County Schools would be swamped with students, but would have an insufficient tax base to cope with the problem. Blount County would have the same problem, although with less severity. Monroe County would contain the majority of the industry and the resulting high tax base. An attempt to operate the school systems under their present conditions would create educational chaos. However, Monroe County should not be expected to share revenue unless the system receives adequate services. The need for an equitable sharing of services and revenue is obvious. The following alternatives are offered: . . . (From a University of Tennessee report of the Little Tennessee Valley Charrette)

Additionally, the financial burden and/or benefits to be felt from the development of the model city were of great concern and importance to the seven school districts.

Stated purposes and intended activities for the Cooperative at its start-up reflect an extension of conflicting interests. Interests of local school districts and those of outside interests were widely divergent. Those with vested interests in the Tellico Project conceived the Co-op as functioning privately within the purposes of planning and development of the Timberlake educational system.

This Utopian idea goes back to the late 1960s when the Tennessee Valley Authority heeded residents' pleas to build a dam on the Little Tennessee River at Lenoir City and otherwise help the sagging economy of the three counties.

TVA didn't just want to build a dam for the sake of building a dam.

It also conceived Timberlake, named for the British explorer who came to these parts in the 1700s. The water-oriented community projected for 50,000 residents would be built to spare citizens from pollution and eyesores from the beginning.

New industry brought in would be located elsewhere. This calls for new vehicle arteries, including new bridges over the Little T (one already has been built), and a school system to take care of today's and tomorrow's children.

PG. 21:

So the Little Tennessee Valley Educational Co-op (LTVEC) was born, supported by joint grants from TVA and the Appalachian Regional Commission. (From News Sentinel, date unknown.)

Certainly, those within the local districts had the needs of their own existing schools, school populations, and programs in mind. The Charrette collected data across the three counties to determine within-county and across-county needs to which LIVE might direct its efforts.

Such a diversity of programs, to be initiated within seven school districts, undoubtedly will require some careful planning and organizing to provide maximum use of the existing facilities, funding, and involvement of resources outside of formal education. Throughout the Charrette a strong desire for cooperation in attempting to solve the educational problems of the Little Tennessee Valley was evident among the citizens, students, and educators alike. An organizational refinement is recommended which might be desirable to improve the cooperative involvement of the seven school systems. (From University of Tennessee Charrette Report.)

It is interesting to note, also, that in the Charrette study the individual counties each reported somewhat different, specialized, and considerably focused needs, which they hoped the co-op might help meet: Blount County, reorganization of high schools, vocational training and sources of funding; Monroe County, new facilities and vocational training; Loudon County, better facility utilization, new educational programs, new sources of funding.

Still, the formal report of the Charrette study was concluded with a broad and inclusive statement of purpose for LIVEC which would parallel that of a typical educational cooperative:

The primary purpose of the Cooperative should be to provide specialized educational services on regional basis so that a high degree of equality in educational opportunity can be achieved and advanced educational practices can be introduced and sustained. The Cooperative should perform those specialized services which school systems are not able to perform efficiently themselves or

PG. 22:

those which could be performed through a pooling of human and material resources. (From University of Tennessee Charrette Report.)

Some of the functions that should be included in the Cooperative would be planning, research, development, evaluation, and services through commonly operated programs of inservice education, vocational education, special education, supplementary media and materials, early childhood education, driver education, educational television, shared teachers and consultants, the use of technological innovations for delivery of programs, and so on. The Tennessee State Department of Education and colleges and universities should participate with the local school systems in responsible roles in the planning and execution of these functions. (From University of Tennessee Charrette Report.)

BUCK ROGERS LAND

"Dr. Oakes called it Buck Rogers Land. It was such an ideal situation: It was real exciting, you know. First of all, there would be a completed educational center for all-aged people... library, swimming pool, golf course . . . idealistic ... classrooms for all nature of the handicapped...a complete educational park for the three counties." (Quote from Glyden Calhoun, Co-op Bookkeeper, 1971 to present.)

At the recommendation of the Charrette, a ten-member Cooperative Board was formed for LTVEC, with one member elected from each of the seven local school boards (Monroe County, Loudon County, Blount County, Sweetwater City, Lenoir City, Alcoa, and Maryville) and one member from each of the three county courts within the Cooperative. In August of 1971, this Board appointed Dr. William Oakes as the LTVEC Executive Director, and the Cooperative began its operations within one year grants from TVA and ARC (Appalachian Regional Commission). Much of the story of the first year or so of operations of LTVEC is related to the character and activities of its new director:

"Bill was a highly verbal person who had wide contacts and went all directions at once. He was

PG. 23:

an idea man...He was a pretty good financial person, fairly well able to hold the Co-op together through personal influence."

"He was local, Knoxville friendly, a wheeler-dealer. He traveled to Washington a lot, and made speeches."

"He was brilliant, committed, but controversial; he wanted to expedite things, didn't always explain...had difficulty explaining, like the budget."

"Bill did not see himself as facilitating local interactions, but interacting with the Department of Labor, the press, TVA, and so on. This first year of the Co-op's operation was intended and funded as a planning and development period. Spirits were high, ideas inspired if at times grandiose, and news releases flowed. Most of the planning at this time was related not to planning of cooperative programs for the seven existing LTVEC school districts, but to the planning and

development of the proposed Human Resources Center to be located at Timberlake, still a dream city."

MADISONVILLE, TN.—There's a sitting-on-the-edge-of-the-chair excitement among educators, public officials, civic leaders and school patrons of this region as they speak of a significant new concept which is being put into operation to meet the educational needs of a three-county area.

A Human Resource Park, opening in 1975, with structures to house a high school, a middle school, and vocational-technical facilities, will involve an initial investment of some $5.2 million for construction on a 300-acre sit northwest of here. The facilities, to serve the residents of Monroe, Blount and Loudon counties, would provide educational training opportunities for all ages.

The program envisions a steady expansion, with additional facilities being constructed over a period of some 25 years, with the total investment

PG. 24:

in buildings, equipment and grounds reaching $32.8 million by some time in the 1990s.

The Human Resource Park could—but would not necessarily--take the place of present high schools operated by the seven school system (some of them municipal) in the three counties. (By Mouzon Peters, Times Tristate Editor.)

Basic educational needs of tri-counties are already apparent, and some possible solutions can be seen. Among these is a perimeter comprehensive high school which could be part of a Human Resource Center (HRC) which would be somewhere near the junction of the three counties, and it is possible that industry and government could become interested and that HRC would develop as a tri-county cultural center. It could include an Area Technical-Vocational School, an Environmental Educational and

Research Center as well as many other facilities and services to serve the young and not-so-young. (Charrette Forum Release, 2/71.)

The Little Tennessee Valley Educational Cooperative (Charrette) is continually searching for alternative means to solve some of the educational and human needs in the area. Of much more modest scope were program efforts, with a few meagre starts especially in vocational training, adult education, and driver education.

Later, in retrospect, Bill Oakes summed up the Cooperative's first year:

"A few programs were started with federal funds, but most of the year was spent pursuing the golden fleece of the future. In September 1972, the fleece began to tarnish and flee further into the future."

LOST DREAMS, BROKEN PROMISES

At this heavily upon point, the identify [identity] of LTVEC still rested [on the] continuing successful development of Timberlake which, in turn, depended on the successful completion of the Tellico Dam (though a few were saying that Timberlake was a good idea with or without the new reservoir). Boeing Corporation had been contracted to spearhead the planning of the residential and industrial components of the model city, and paralleling the Co-op's first year of operation, Boeing had correspondingly invested $250,000 in their

PG. 25:

part of the overall Timberlake effort. Meanwhile, public sentiment and other antagonistic forces were gaining support in their fight against the construction of the Tellico Dam. TVA, therefore, had become extremely reluctant to follow through with its early promises of support, especially economic support to the Timberlake project or to the Co-operative.

Boeing finally withdrew entirely, leaving the Timberlake Project essentially without direction and support, and leaving LIVEC in a seemingly helpless situation, as well; essentially without support, identity, and--most important--without a dream or a cause. The situation is summarized in the following LTVEC Board Meeting Notes:

> *Evaluations of LTVEC and TVA—It was pointed out to the board that there seems a distinct possibility that Timberlake will not develop at the previously envisioned rate, and it may be 1980 before significant numbers of Timberlake residents are on hand. Since the needs of the tri-county area have existed for some time, it is obvious a delay of another eight years or so would not be appropriate. The Board then discussed the possibility of returning to the original recommendations of the Charrette and exploring the possibilities of a perimeter high school, a Special Education facility, and a state area voc-tech school.*

As these minutes reflect, LTVEC realized its only option for survival was to recoup forces, focus inwardly, and find within its own ranks of seven school districts the individual and cooperative needs which would provide their mutual commitment with a real purpose and an action agenda.

Paradoxically, perhaps, the withdrawal of external support from TVA and Boeing provided Co-op membership with the start of a new identity, of a sort, or perhaps the return to an old identity that was there all along, before Timberlake and all the rest, not formalized as the Little Tennessee Valley Cooperative, but there as a loosely-coupled network of local people with local concerns, who stood sometimes apart and sometimes together for things which they cared about--like their children, their families, their property, their independence, their simpler life style, their right to being slow to commit but long in commitment. When the odds were against them, the rugged individualism for which their southern and mountain ancestors have so long been known stood the Co-op well in turning the corner in their affair with TVA. Or as one Board member has said:

PG. 26:

"Then the thrust went inward. It was Oakes. Plus the fact that there's a stubbornness in the Tennessee personality that says, 'By Goerge, we're gonna make it work whether it's with TVA or not.'"

This transition was not to be an easy one, however, and found the cooperative entering into a long and painful struggle toward redirection, autonomy and self-sufficiency.

As the last of the TVA and ARC grant monies were coming available, a new ARC grant in the amount of $65,000 was negotiated. The new grant was months in gaining the go-ahead from ARC central offices, leaving LTVEC in increasingly extenuating financial circumstances. Board notes of November 15, 1972, reflect the worsening situation:

There apparently comes a time in the life of each cooperative when the lag between expenditures and receipt of a federal check forces the cooperative movement in most states, unless they are directly supported by the state Department of Education. Our present cash balance is zero. The first payment on our TVA contract will come after the first of the month, and we still have $3,900.00 coming from last year's ARC contract. In the meantime we need a bank loan.

Rapidly depleting funds and high overhead costs led the co-op in the spring of 1973 to move from its location in Greenback to empty space in ALCOA School District. When the ARC grant monies finally came available, the total amount was reduced substantially from the original budget, due to an agency policy which disallowed retroactive reimbursements.

Salary checks were delayed for weeks, the Co-op found itself burdened with a debt it had no resources to repay and morale hit a new low. Glynden Calhoun described the final page of this rather dismal chapter in the life of the Co-op as follows:

"In '73, when we moved up to ALCOA, there was not much more activity.

We couldn't keep going on promises. We had to have money....So long as Timberlake was being planned, there was enthusiasm. There was TVA with all their money. And Boeing. And ARC...[But there were] growing pains. You can't sit still. I've heard Dr. Oaks say, "You have to grow or give up."

For more than a year, the Co-op was engaged in an active struggle for survival, an almost day-to-day battle to create a new identify [identity], to set new and realistic goals, and to

PG. 27:

become financially solvent. As a strong resentment developed against the fickleness of outside forces and agencies; a considerable moral investment was made by Bill Oakes and Board members in somehow finding ways to become self-sufficient.

During this period, Board membership, previously including only school board and county court members, was enlarged to include superintendents from the seven school districts.

This change modified the governance and undoubtedly the vision of the Board from one of more general political interests (and perhaps somewhat limited commitment) to greater investment in school-related issues.

The Co-op had maintained a poor record, to this date, in development of effective new programs. It had placed minimal investment of resources into a smorgasbord of programs for the district, none of which seemed particularly vital or of high priority to anyone.

Bill Oakes realized that the Co-op needed a new central and motivating theme which could somehow generate both enthusiasm and funds for Co-op operations. A first opportunity of this sort occurred with the Co-op's attempts to develop a viable vocational educational program. Voc Ed seemed a likely lifeboat; two years before, the Charrette had listed it as a top priority need across all three counties. Even more important now, the state was currently making plans for support of planning and development of new vocational education centers across the state. The hope was that LTVEC might assume administrative responsibility for a cooperative Voc Ed program effort among the seven school districts. The outcome of state Voc Tech plans, however, was that the state finally provided the physical structures but not monetary support for program development, so, in the end, the various districts developed their own Voc Tech programs without LIVEC.

Concurrently, the emergence of an all-important program, psychological services, had later begun to emerge as a program to hold a central place over several years in the purpose, vitality, and services of LTVEC. Paradoxically, it seems, the full potential of the program was not at first clearly perceived, as can be seen in the following rather perfunctory summary appearing in "Cooperatively Speaking," an LTVEC newsletter:

LTVEC's last bucket of money from the federal well has been approved, and, with this, programs for the school year 1973-74 have been planned

PG. 28:

and submitted to the respective Boards of Education. A serious problem for years has been the lack of being able to test students to determine the programs they need. Such a program is called psychological services, and LTVEC has proposed to provide the service.

A school psychologist has been found, and, with interns from UT and help from the State Department of Education, screening of students is proposed to begin in September, 1873 [1973].

BETTER YEARS

With 1973 dawned the beginning of a new era for the Co-op. That year, Tennessee Public Law 839 came into effect along with additional state funding to hasten compliance. The law established as state policy to require school districts to provide special education services sufficient to meet the needs and maximize the capabilities of handicapped children.

This new mandate loomed large and threatening for most school districts. First, the state did not interpret the law, nor did it prescribe the logistics of how compliance might occur. Secondly, the educational implications of the law ran contrary to the existing fabric of schooling being practiced by many districts. As one observer put it, "The law was antithetical to the educational system in the state—a bureaucracy in which educators run the show.

The seven LTVEC districts were sufficiently alarmed about the prospects of the new legislation for educating the handicapped to agree to the cooperative pooling of resources in order that the Co-op might develop a full-scale psychological service program, complete with an added staff person to see to its success. Subsequently, this person, Dr. Jerry Morton, was hired. He immediately embarked upon a mission to successfully utilize the Handicapped Education Law, with its encumbrances and benefits, as a vehicle for pulling the Cooperative together, strengthening programs, enlarging staff, balancing the budget, and shaping a new dream for the Co-op, a dream which was to include words like "individualized instruction," "advocacy for children," "development of human resources," and "educational revolution."

Claire Brown, the on-site evaluator, operated out of a motel room in Blount County for eighteen days in March 1979 while she interviewed and collected other information to enable their report to be written. As noted, the report was published and provided to LTVEC in August 1979.

The study's account of the funding shortfall is referenced on page 26 of the report. The study notes that the shortfall forced the cooperative to obtain a bank loan in 1972. That relating of events differs somewhat from an oral account given me around 1985 by the then-chairman of LTVEC's Board of Directors, Billy Joe Littleton. According to Billy Joe, TVA was to provide the cooperative $60,000 to pay the administrative expenses during the 1972-1973 school year. When Bill Oakes completed the grant and submitted it to TVA in the early summer of 1972, TVA told him that he needed to rewrite it in order to meet their specific requirements for grant submissions. He did and resubmitted it a little while later. Again, TVA said it still did not meet their requirements. The grant needed to be rewritten again. By this time the cooperative became worried that TVA might not fund the full $60,000. The fear was that TVA would declare that the grant would only fund the year from the point in time at which the grant was approved. According to Billy Joe, TVA assured the board that the grant would be funded the full amount, $60,000, once the paperwork had been approved.

With that assurance, three individuals decided to take out personal loans in the amount of ten thousand dollars each, to cover the administrative costs until the TVA grant was officially approved. Billy Joe said that he, Bill Oakes and Frank McClellan, then chairman of the co-op's board, obtained personal loans from their local banks to provide thirty thousand dollars to cover the operational costs of LTVEC with the understanding that TVA would soon fund the cooperative the full sixty-thousand-dollar grant. LTVEC would then repay the board members. When the grant was finally approved in the middle of the school year, it was for thirty thousand dollars. When TVA was confronted with the fact that LTVEC had been assured that the grant would be for the full sixty thousand dollars, TVA officials regretted that LTVEC had misunderstood what TVA officials had said. However, they stated, TVA never pays out grant funds retroactively before the grant's approval date.

LTVEC was faced with a thirty-thousand-dollar debt and no known way to pay it. I am not sure how the loan was paid back, but it was. By the time I became the director in January 1976, it had been paid. That was when I became responsible for the entire financial condition of the organization. My guess is that the funds necessary for the reimbursement to the three supporters were collected as part of the membership fees charged to the seven member systems.

FOUR
INTERVIEW BY THE BOARD

My employment interview with the full board of directors was in the late spring of 1973. Prior to that interview, Bill and I had met several times as the plans for delivering the new services were developed. He had provided me with a copy of the state's new special education law, which I had thoroughly studied. We determined how much funding would be available for me to hire others, what could be expected of the services to be provided that first year and how we would ensure each system would receive its fair share of the overall services provided through the cooperative. I refer to Dr. Oakes as Bill, for we quickly became friends. It was a true honor to be mentored by him for the two and a half years we were together. His accidental death in December 1975, was a great sadness to me and many others. That was when I became the overall director of the cooperative's operations.

What an unusual experience the interview with the LTVEC Board of Directors was that late spring evening! The board met in the basement of a small branch bank in Vonore. The chairman of the Board was Dr. Frank McClellan, dean of Maryville College. He was also the county commissioner representing the Blount County

Commission. My mind does not retain the names of the various superintendents, school board members, or other county commissioners.

I was to wait in Bill's car until the board of directors was ready to interview me. Bill said that he would provide the board with my background information and my plans for creating a delivery of services model with the funds that they would provide.

With Bill's guidance, I had developed a comprehensive plan for getting the best delivery of services with the funds we thought would be available. I was going to recruit graduate assistants from the University of Tennessee doctoral school psychology program, which was a joint program between the university's psychology and educational psychology departments. At that time, the going rate for a doctoral graduate assistant/school psychology intern working twenty hours a week was $4,000, plus mileage. I would direct the graduate students and provide additional training to them as needed. I would also be involved in testing and evaluating the more complex cases that might arise in any member system.

In addition, there would be one full-time special education professional to conduct training to teachers throughout the member school systems. Up to this point, none of the teachers had been oriented to the many requirements placed upon general education to serve special needs children in the regular classrooms or trained in how to implement those requirements effectively. I would assist in the teacher training process as well with a particular emphasis on positive behavioral intervention strategies. For those educators interested, I would also provide training in a developmental play strategy designed to assist teachers working with children who had serious behavior problems. I had had extensive experience in these activities in the St. Petersburg, Florida, schools. My dissertation research had established the value of this intervention process.

The size of the bank building where the meeting was to be held was a surprise. It was so small. The building sat starkly on the side of U.S. 411 in a sparse scattering of commercial buildings near the

Highway 411 bridge crossing the Little Tennessee River. The walk down the narrow stairwell with Bill into the building's basement was full of excitement for me. The stairs led us into a conference room off a small hallway. The board members were seated around the three sides of tables pushed together to form a rectangle. Two empty chairs sat at the top of the rectangle nearest the stairwell. Bill motioned for me to sit in one of the chairs; he proceeded to sit in the other.

All the board members appeared to be around Bill's age or older. By appearance, Dr. McClellan, the chairman, was the oldest person in the room. He made a very distinguished appearance. The board members' attire suggested that they represented a diverse mixture of backgrounds. A few superintendents from the member systems were not in attendance although most of the elected school board members and county commissioners were. A couple of the men wore white shirts and ties as I did. Several wore open-collar shirts that had been well pressed. A few of the board members were dressed more casually. One member looked like my great-uncle Edward coming home to supper after a long day's work in the fields of his farm back in Ohio.

In my excitement, I knew that the names and positions of the board members presented to me would never anchor themselves in my mind that evening. However, I did note that the man who reminded me of my uncle Edward was a school board member from the Monroe County School System.

Questions flowed from the board members concerning my understanding of the new special education law. In response to those questions, I noted that I had had the opportunity to study the law in its entirety. I thought it was just what was needed to assist regular classroom teachers in helping many of the struggling students already in their classrooms. My experiences in the St. Petersburg and Knoxville City Schools demonstrated to me the large number of children with learning disabilities and emotional problems currently among the students in a regular classroom. The lack of resources to assist classroom teachers in addressing the educational needs of these children was extremely frustrating to the teachers and a major hindrance to the affected children as they tried to learn what the teacher was teaching. We, as educators, had often experienced seeing those children fail, become discouraged and simply fade away as school dropouts. In the coming school year, we could make significant steps in stopping this sad cycle.

The new special education law provided some funding for specialists to be employed by the school systems to set up special programs for learning-disabled and emotionally troubled youth. Not all of those programs required the removal of these children from the regular classroom for part or all of the day. A classroom teacher could implement fairly straightforward strategies with many of these children without interfering with her overall classroom teaching strategies. The law also allowed for funds to be spent to provide aides in the classroom to assist those special education children.

Up to this point, the vast majority of working teachers had not been trained in these strategies or made aware of state-of–the-art research for assisting these children. That's where professionals, trained as I was, could be of great assistance. We knew how to identify the children with the various disabilities the law mandated be addressed and how to address many of those disabilities.

I was prepared for the questions I received as to how I could manage employing graduate assistants from the school psychology doctoral program in such a way that they would be able to determine which children had what disabilities and make recommendations for implementing the necessary intervention strategies.

The answers I provided to the board revolved around my unique position in the doctoral program at the university. I was a member of the first group of graduate students to be admitted into the newly created doctoral school psychology program. I was the only entering student with a master's degree in school psychology, the only one with two years of experience functioning as a master's level school psychologist in public schools that were actively engaged in major changes. I was also the only one with two years' experience in routinely instructing large groups of military officers on issues concerning social change in populations experiencing high levels of stress. As a result of my master's degree, my work as a school psychologist and my work in psychology while in the army, I was in the process of completing the doctorate in two years rather than the normal seven years expected of my fellow graduate students. I knew the training they were receiving. It was ideal preparation for school psychologists in the roles they were to fulfill at LTVEC. In addition, I knew which of the graduate students had the most highly developed skills and possessed those intangible qualities necessary for relating to teachers encountering stressful changes. I was confident that we could be of significant assistance to the school systems' educators in fulfilling the requirements of the law.

The non-verbal feedback the various board members were displaying suggested that they were in agreement with my answers. I was feeling more and more confident about being offered the position until the farmer/county school board member asked me what my opinions were concerning educational strategies to use with hearing-impaired and deaf students.

Deaf education was not an area of my studies. Informally, I had interacted with the head of the university's deaf education department a little and had become friends with a young department faculty member, John Berry, doing cutting-edge research in collaboration with researchers in Europe. I knew a little about that research as a result of my friendship with him.

My response to the board member's question concerning children with hearing problems was shallow. I acknowledged a lack of in-depth knowledge in the field while noting that there were specialists at the university who were more than willing to provide assistance to the schools in this area. I concluded my answer by stating that many professionals in various specialized fields would need to be engaged in order to meet the specific disabling conditions various children had.

"Yes," he replied, "but what do you know about the verbal-tonal approach to assisting children with hearing problems?"

This question brought a big smile to my face as I replied, "Well, I suspect that you know, John Berry at UT, is doing some cutting-edge research of the verbal-tonal method and how it enables hearing disabled children to be taught in a regular classroom environment."

Maintaining my smile, I went on to say, "I suspect you know a lot more about this approach than I do."

"Well, my grandson is in their verbal-tonal program. It has helped him a lot. It's my hope that the educational cooperative will be helping get this program going in one of our schools so that he can attend regular school."

"I think that would be outstanding," came my spontaneous response.

With that, Dr. Oakes, Bill, asked if there were any more questions. Concluding that the board's questions to me were completed, he directed me to return to his car while the board deliberated on my application. After a few minutes had passed, Bill joined me to announce that I was now an employee of LTVEC. I would start working on July 1.

On the drive back to the Alcoa offices that night, Bill informed me that the farmer board member liked to come across as a good old boy to strangers to see if they would act condescendingly to him. That's how he would get the measure of the person. My response to his question was perfect. I had not fallen into his trap. The guy was a highly regarded national expert in the breeding of a unique genetic line of cattle and was currently the president of the farmers' association for the state.

The lessons I had learned over my career concerning the importance of valuing people from different cultures would be applied often in assisting the graduate assistants and myself during those early years of the cooperative.

FIVE
THE FIRST TASK

Events don't always unfold as we had envisioned. Such was the case with my dissertation and the cooperative. As a result of a misunderstanding, my doctoral committee missed the deadline for submitting documentation that I had completed the doctoral program requirements. I was not able to receive my degree in August 1973. I would have to wait until December.

Bill Oakes was not concerned about the delay. I met the qualifications for being certified as a school psychologist by the Tennessee State Department of Education. The psychology department indicated that I was qualified to supervise doctoral level school psychology graduate assistants. In January 1974, I met all of the requirements to apply for licensure as a psychologist with a specialty in school psychology with the Tennessee Board of Healing Arts and did become licensed in addition to being certified by the Tennessee Department of Education.

Thanks to Bill's understanding of the situation, I had a degree of flexibility in my July work schedule. This allowed me to effectively conclude my last-minute doctoral duties with the university. Until the end of December, I would still have to be a registered student in the doctoral program. I was required to pay the university for carrying additional dissertation hours. Fortunately, my GI educational support continued as a result of that enrollment. Those payments helped ease the financial burden of paying the university fees.

Early in July, Bill called me into his office to say something like, "Jerry, we have a problem. Our seven school systems have yet to finalize their contracts with the cooperative for the school psychological services we planned to provide. We will be meeting with all seven superintendents next week to get their firm commitment to provide us with the promised funds. It would help if you met with every superintendent before that meeting to re-explain how we are going to use each system's funds to create and manage the delivery of psychological services to their system as well as to the other member systems. The superintendents are afraid that some of their money will be used to provide services to one of the other school systems. You will be able to re-assure them that this is not the case."

Since Bill and I had already devised a strategy to ensure that one school system's funding would not be used to pay for services another system received, I did not perceive a problem in meeting this request. My problem was that I did not know who the seven superintendents were or where their offices were located. Another problem that was hard for me to face was my unease about interacting with school superintendents. They were the key authority figures. Remembering being in elementary school, high school, college and graduate school knowing that I was just a lowly student and they were the biggest of the big placed a heavy weight upon me emotionally. Up to this time, to me, superintendents had represented punishment. As a student, you wanted to avoid them at all costs.

At the time, I realized that I had successfully interacted with many senior authority figures in the past. Twice I had to appear before the commanding general of the special warfare center to face a complaint filed against me. In one complaint, the senior officer, a colonel, of a class I was instructing objected to a point I was making.

Once the general understood what I had said, he supported my position. There were other similar situations in other organizations where I was supported by the chief authority figure. Logically, my feelings of intimidation from education authority figures were not warranted. However, they were real feelings. I had to shake off the cultural weight of the educational authoritarian role model if I was to accomplish the goals of the cooperative.

The three member counties of the cooperative covered a large geographical area. I doubted that it was possible to drive from one edge of the landmass to the other in a workday, let alone to make all the visits necessary. Further complicating traveling from one superintendent's office to another was the lack of road signs. There was a deficit of signs that told you what rural road you were currently driving on although there were plenty of signs telling you what road you could make a right or left turn onto. I got lost a lot trying to drive from one school system's central office to another. This was frustrating because I had set appointment times to meet with each superintendent.

In my first meeting with a superintendent, it became apparent that he did not understand the immediate requirements of the law to evaluate children for the purpose of determining if they qualified for special education services. I learned that up until this point, when all but the major city school systems wanted a child to be evaluated by a psychologist about a school-related issue, the system contacted someone in the state capital, Nashville. The state department of education would send a licensed psychologist to the system to conduct the evaluation. The Department of Education made a direct payment to the psychologist for the evaluation. Sometimes the selected psychologist was located more than a hundred miles from the school building in which the evaluation was conducted.

Once the report from the psychologist was sent to the school system, the school system decided if it would provide the child with special services. That special service focused on placing the child in a program or class that had been created years before and currently had an opening. More often than not, the system decided that it could not serve the child. Therefore, the child could not attend school. To their credit, some of the rural school systems provided a few special education services. For example, a system might have three or four classes, classrooms, designated for moderately retarded children. "Retarded" was a socially accepted term in 1973. If a child was more "retarded" than the system felt it could serve, the system simply told the parents the child could not attend school. This model of psychological services dominated the thinking of the educators in the cooperative's region, including the superintendents. They did not understand the depth of services a comprehensive delivery model of school psychology could provide nor the demands of special services they were required to provide. A relatively small number of Tennessee's school systems had special education centers serving severely disabled children. Typically, children with severe physical disabilities would be attending these centers. Those children who had to be in wheelchairs or suffered from severe brain damage or acute autistic symptoms were the ones usually attending such centers.

A key misunderstanding held by the superintendents and their subordinates concerned the concept of special education services. To them, special education services meant having specialized programs ready to serve children who fit the requirements of those programs. This concept conflicted with the intent of the new Tennessee Special Education law. The law focused on building individualized special education service around the needs of each identified child.

It was clear in my first interview with a superintendent that I needed to explain the nature of comprehensive school psychological services, the intent of the special education law in identifying a qualified disability, and the necessity to determine to what extent a child's regular education would have to be adjusted in order for the child to receive an appropriate education.

The most pressing concern articulated by the majority of superintendents was that at least some of the money provided to the cooperative would be used to provide services to children in other school systems. They feared that other school systems would try to influence the cooperative's administration to the detriment of their children. In short, the member school systems did not trust one another. Many of the school systems were in competition with neighboring systems to prove to their voters that their leadership, their school system, was better than the surrounding ones.

I quickly realized that my task in meeting with each of the superintendents was far more complicated than simply convincing them to use their special education evaluation allotments to fund school psychological services through LTVEC. I had to assist them in understanding what the new model for serving all children with disabilities was, how the cooperative would ensure their funding would be used only for their children and how the psychological services model was critical to their meeting the new requirements.

Superintendents are busy professionals. Spending a half-hour in a one-on-one meeting constitutes a long meeting for the majority of them. My meeting with them was going to be a lengthy affair if I were to cover all the information they needed to know. At the end of each meeting during that week, I felt that the superintendents understood our plan to ensure that their money would be used only for their children. I also felt I had assured them that Bill Oakes and I would be able to resist pressure from other member systems to deviate from this plan.

In each meeting, the time pressures on the superintendent was such that I was never confident that they understood the difference between a child with an identified disability who did not need special education services, a child who needed simple classroom adjustments in order for their educational needs to be meet, a child who needed to receive some specialized services outside the classroom part of a day and the child who needed specialized services all day every day. Understanding the difference between developing and delivering an individualized program for a child as contrasted to simply placing the child in a generic special education program was another difficult concept to communicate in the time frame allotted me with each superintendent.

By the meeting time scheduled for the cooperative's superintendents to announce their decision concerning their contracts with LTVEC, I felt fairly confident that they understood the cooperative's plan for the delivery of school psychological services. However, I did not know if all, some or none of them intended to participate in the program. The details of the program were interwoven with the requirements of the new special education law. For those encountering the requirements for the first time, the actions that needed to take place were complex.

An explanation of some of the new requirements will reveal the level of complexity encountered by those who believed that special education's role had always been to simply take disabled children out of the regular classroom and place them in some kind of a program. In turn, the plan for assuring the school systems that they would receive their fair share of psychological services through the cooperative needs to be thoroughly explained.

We all understood the state department of education's plan for funding this first year of implementing the law. The state was providing one dollar per child enrolled in a school system for the purpose of identifying all children with qualifying disabilities, and then of developing plans for meeting the educational needs of those children. The state did not plan to actually provide additional funding for delivering new special education services to the systems until the following year.

To a school system of fifty thousand students, a dollar a child was a lot of money in 1973. However, a dollar per child for a system of one thousand two hundred students couldn't do much in establishing comprehensive testing services. Pooling resources through the educational cooperative model was an excellent solution for its member school systems. In this way, they could all provide the necessary psychological evaluations with the funding provided them.

In order for a child to receive special education services funded by the state, the child had to have one of the state's qualifying disabilities, and that qualifying disability had to be negatively interfering with the effectiveness of the child's regular educational program. To most educators, this meant that if the regular classroom instruction didn't produce normal progress in a child with a disability, then some educational changes needed to be made. Those educational adjustments needed to take place in as normal a classroom environment as possible.

I thought all of the superintendents understood the cooperative's school psychology delivery model. The plan included employing me as the supervising school psychologist. In turn, I would employ senior graduate students as graduate assistants from the University of Tennessee's doctoral school psychology program to work in the participating school systems. Each school system would receive the same percentage of school psychology services hours as they paid into the cooperative for these services when compared to the total amount of money provided to the cooperative by the member systems. Each school system would receive regular reports of the various school psychological services provided to its system as well as records of the services provided to the other systems. The percentages of the services provided to each school system when compared to the total amount of services provided would be compiled on a monthly basis and presented to the LTVEC board of directors at the monthly board of directors' meetings. Any monthly discrepancies between actual percentages of services provided a school system above or below the contracted percentage of services would be explained with the anticipation that there would be appropriate corrections in the coming months. It had been established earlier that there would have to be in-service training for teachers and staff about the special education law. The law would require new educational strategies on the part of many teachers. Those in-services were included in the definition of school psychological services. Depending on the funds made available to the cooperative, an educational specialist would be employed to assist in this task.

The week before the cooperative's decisive meeting with the seven school systems went fast for me. Constantly getting lost on the back roads of our rural counties caused me to arrive late to some meetings. At that time the interstate highway connecting Knoxville and Chattanooga was not complete. The fastest route for me to travel from Alcoa to Sweetwater included driving several miles on a one-lane dirt and gravel road. I learned about that shortcut from verbal instructions that I did not fully understand. I got to see a lot of beautiful countryside finding that gravel road. The standing jokes about how instructions for getting from one place to another were given included, "You're not from around here are you?" and "You go down here a ways then turn left by that red barn that burned down a while back."

A few of the superintendents became impatient with the time it was taking to cover all of the information I felt they needed to know. I pressed the issue. The information was necessary if they were to make an informed decision about funding the cooperative's proposal. The day before the big meeting, I had my last superintendent conference. It was with the superintendent of the largest system in the cooperative. He had missed the last cooperatives' board of directors meeting, the meeting of my interview. Without this system's participation I was not sure we could develop the comprehensive program I envisioned.

At last, the final day had arrived. A large former classroom of the old Alcoa High School served as the cooperative's conference room. It appeared that all of the superintendents were present. Several superintendents had brought key staff members with them. People were standing throughout the room in clumps talking to each other, waiting for Bill to call the meeting to order. I seemed to be the only one all by himself. There was no one there that I really knew outside of Bill. He was deeply engaged with a couple of administrators. I didn't want to just barge in and disrupt their flow of conversation. Then I noticed a new arrival. He stood by the entrance to the room looking around.

Walking up to him, I held out my hand as I displayed a big smile saying, "Hi, I'm Jerry Morton with LTVEC. I don't believe I've had the chance to meet you."

"Why, yes you have," he said with a nodding smile.

"I'm sorry sir, but I don't think we have."

"Come on," he exclaimed with a puzzled look, "We met in my office yesterday. I'm Leroy Goodin, superintendent of the county's schools."

"What a fool I must appear to be," flashed across my mind as I replied, "Oh, yes. I'm so sorry. It's just that I have been meeting so many new people in such a short time," I stammered out as I thought, "I have just blown away the biggest school system in the cooperative."

Laughing, with his eyes twinkling, he replied, "I'm glad to see it happens to other people, too. This constantly greeting new people kind of gets to you, doesn't it?"

I nodded vigorously as we both chuckled.

The announcement was made; the meeting started.

Under the conditions described, all seven-school systems decided to provide funding to LTVEC for school psychological services. Some of the school systems designated all of the funds the state provided for LTVEC's school psychological services while others used some of the money for other purposes. In total, LTVEC had about one hundred thousand dollars for the services with the largest school system providing about forty thousand dollars and the smallest system putting in around five thousand dollars.

SIX
GETTING STARTED

The entire process was new to all of the participants. The cooperative's school systems had never been able to create a delivery of school psychological services for themselves and did not have a working concept of the value of such a service for meeting the educational needs of children with disabilities. The graduate assistants about to develop the school psychology services delivery model for these schools had never been involved in the creation of psychological services to school systems that lacked a working concept as to what the services could do for their system, their teachers and their children.

As far as I could tell, there had never been an effective effort in the state of Tennessee for school systems to cooperate across their political boundaries in delivering direct services to their teachers and children outside of its recent passage of a law allowing school systems to form agreements with other school systems to create cooperative organizations. That was the law that allowed the creation of LTVEC. Most Tennessee school systems had never created a comprehensive delivery system for children with disabilities. Their common practice was to tell the parents with children having obvious disabilities that they were sorry, but they did not service children with those disabilities. The children were denied an education. It was also true that my tasks with the cooperative were new to me. However, I did have some unique experiences that provided me with insights into working as a school psychologist with individuals, schools and organizations experiencing significant changes and in training those who would be facilitating those changes.

As I mentioned earlier, my two years of being a school psychologist in the seven all-black inner-city schools of St. Petersburg, Florida, were a first for those schools. Any school psychological services those schools had received before my arrival would have been very minimal. At the time I was working there, it had never occurred to me to ask how much, if any, school psychological services had been provided before the grants to the system allowed for the expansion my presence represented. In any event, my experiences there provided me with multiple firsts. Those opportunities of introducing new strategies for assisting educators to develop and implement heretofore untried interventions in facilitating the learning experiences of their children gave me confidence in accomplishing the tasks before me.

The Pinellas County, Florida, School System provided me and their other school psychologists with excellent continuing education training. The system sent me, along with others, to a two-week summer training program that allowed me to develop my skills as a group facilitator. Several of us led bi-racial groups of educators and community leaders as they were in the process of integrating their communities. The effectiveness of these strategies was such that my colleagues and I were conducting in-service training sessions at regional and statewide professional conferences on a regular basis. In turn, the support provided to me from the other professional school psychologists employed by the system was outstanding. We problem-solved together, shared successes and assisted each other in implementing strategies to help the children. We were all part of a highly caring and effective support team.

When a child's difficulties were such that our intervention strategies failed, the system provided us with training from professionals involved in developing research on new strategies for assisting children with difficulties. These experiences enabled me to become highly skilled in implementing various positive reinforcement strategies and developmental play therapies.

My three years in the Army provided me with the understanding and the skills focused on the role of the change agent in situations of high stress for people from various cultures. After a year of Army training, I had invaluable experiences as a psychology instructor at the Psychological Warfare School, JFK Special Warfare Center, Ft. Bragg, North Carolina. I had just completed my master's degree in school psychology days before the draft system forced me into the Army. I'm sure that the master's degree helped the Army decide to assign me there.

Once again, I learned the importance of understanding the perspective of those with whom you were trying to communicate, why one needed to value the point of view of those who disagreed with you, and the overriding emotional investment all humans have in believing they are the hero of their own stories. Rather than attacking the behavior of those you are trying to assist to behave differently, it is critical that the change agent focus on assisting the target audience to change their understanding of the situation. Once someone's interpretation of the situation changes, their behavior will naturally change so that their concept of being a just and good person is maintained.

To my surprise, the training I received to become a practicing school psychologist was perfect in preparing for this role. As a consultant to a teacher in making adjustments to her classroom instructional role to better assist various children, it was important to value the teacher, her sense of worth, as you were assisting her in learning new strategies to help her students learn and interact with others. The Army experience re-emphasized for me the importance of being congruent. Your words have to be congruent with what you mean when you say something. Your behavior has to be congruent with what you say. If you ask a teacher to be eighty percent positive in her corrective instructions to a student, you have to be eighty percent positive in your coaching of her as she implements new educational and behavioral strategies.

I gained a deeper understanding of this concept and expanded upon it as I wrote and then taught over one thousand hours of classes a year to military officers. The extensive experience of speaking before large groups of people was the perfect preparation for me to conduct in-service training sessions to educators and graduate students in my new role at the educational cooperative.

Additional experiences that helped prepare me for the tasks to be accomplished through the educational cooperative included my doctoral training program at the University of Tennessee and the graduate assistantship I had with the Knoxville City School System during my second and last year as a doctoral graduate student. In addition to the newest research in the development of school psychological services at the university, there was a focus on systems analysis. This focus provided me and the other graduate students with insights into implementing system change strategies, evaluating the effectiveness of those strategies and making adjustments to those activities as needed. Being able to determine quickly what was effective or ineffective in assisting a system to respond to mandatory changes was of considerable value for the accomplishment of the tasks before us.

Since I was a fellow graduate student with the others in the school psychology program, I had some insights into understanding which ones of them might serve as excellent change agents in introducing all of the mandatory changes the school systems and their professional staff would have to make. When we were all together, I would sometimes refer to them as the cooperative's special ops cadre.

From the school system's perspective, their educators were being confronted with revolutionary concepts. For the first time in their history, the school systems were required to provide special education services to all children who were correctly identified as disabled. Those special services had to meet very specific standards. Those standards included providing the services within the regular classroom where appropriate.

Fortunately, the state had selected me to be among a small group of educators to write its new rules and regulations for implementation of the law. The next year, the 1974-1975 school year, I was appointed to be one of the state's due process hearing officers. A due process hearing officer was the one who heard both sides of a contested issue concerning the appropriateness of the educational program a school system was proposing for a child with a disability when the parents disagreed with the proposal. This appointment allowed me to be trained in the state and national laws regarding special education.

The training included studying all of the significant court cases that were being adjudicated across the country as soon as the rulings were made public. I was a due process hearing officer from 1974 through 1985. I would take vacation days to serve in that role, and I could not hear a case from a school system that might present me with a conflict of interest. The excellence of the training we all received was reflected in the fact that during those eleven years, none of our rulings were ever overturned by a state or federal court.

If the system was going to remove a child with a disability from the regular classroom in order to meet the child's educational needs, the system had to have documented reasons for doing so. The parameters of those actions were carefully described within the new law. Simply because a child needed to receive a specialized service outside of the regular classroom in order to meet his educational goals was not a reason to keep that child out of the regular school program for the whole day. Each degree of separation of a child from his regular classroom program had to be justified.

The new law was actually a civil rights issue. Every child with a disability had the right to receive a free and appropriate education. If the system was going to violate that right, treat a child differently than other children, the system had to have documented reasons for doing so. In turn, the system had to document that the child was educationally benefiting from the intervention. To ensure that the educational plan met the unique needs of a child with disabilities, the child's plan was to be created by a multi-disciplinary team, an M-Team.

The M-Team included the child's regular classroom teacher, the assessment specialist, the specialists needed for the services to be provided to the child and the child's parents. To ensure that the child's educational rights were not violated, the school system provided parents with information about those rights as well as how to appeal any decisions made by the M-Team. That appeal process included how to request that a due process hearing be conducted.

A due process hearing was a step just below a formal court of law appearance. An independent professional who had been trained in both the delivery of educational services and the special education law would be assigned by the state of Tennessee to hear the positions of the parents and the school system on the appropriateness of the educational plan for the child. Attorneys could represent both parties if they wished. A court recorder would record all testimony that was given by various individuals that the contesting parties desired to have testify in the hearing. Once the hearing officer had made a written decision in the case, both parties had the right to appeal that decision to a state or federal court, depending on which jurisdiction was applicable.

The school systems were confronted with a new accountability system that was definitely threatening to many. Not only were they required to implement a totally unfamiliar educational structure into their regular educational program, they were now going to be held accountable for the success of that new structure on a child-by-child basis.

The anxiety level of teachers who were already experiencing stress due to a lack of full funding for their schools was definitely being raised. Many of the rural schools did not have enough textbooks for all of their children. What textbooks they did have were outdated in areas such as biology, history, and social studies. Additionally, many of the schools lacked basic teaching supplies for teachers and students, the classrooms were overcrowded and there was a major lack of funding for trained staff in areas such as counselors, nurses, speech and language therapists, vision specialists and on and on.

Adding to the anxiety within the school systems concerning this new law was a basic misunderstanding by a large number of school administrators and teaching staff who did not fully grasp the changes that were being imposed on them. Most staff at the building level had received little or no information about the changes they were expected to implement. A large number of educators were so convinced that the law would be impossible to implement that they believed the state's legislators would repeal it. As one high-level system administrator explained to me a few years after the law was implemented, "The only reason our school system let the cooperative be in charge of school psych services was that we knew the special ed. law would be repealed in a couple of years. No one wanted it. It was bad law. It would go away. If we had known then how important school psych. services were going to be, we would never have allowed the cooperative to set it up."

I was pleased to be in my new position with the cooperative. I thought the law was just what the teachers needed to assist them in helping so many of their children who were just sitting in their classrooms failing. The teachers I had worked with in St. Petersburg and Knoxville wanted to help those children. They just did not have the time to invest in meeting the needs of the failing students while continuing to meet the needs of the successful children. At last, the teachers were going to find out what the learning problems of the troubled children were and receive professional support in finding ways to better help those children while being engaged with multiple professionals on behalf of the children with disabilities.

My tasks, through the cooperative, were multiple. The first step was to employ the most qualified assessment specialists, school psychologists, I could with the funds available to me. As mentioned before, this meant employing advanced graduate students in the school psychology doctoral program as graduate assistants that I would mentor and supervise. I needed to be certain that the graduate assistants had the necessary training to evaluate the children's difficulties, make appropriate recommendations for adopting strategies to address those difficulties and evaluate the benefits of those interventions. Even if a referred child's difficulties did not meet the requirements of the state for services funded with special education dollars, the graduate assistant needed to make recommendations to assist the teacher in helping the child. Since the graduate assistant was not going to be the educator to do the specialized teaching a child with a disability required, the graduate assistant needed excellent consulting skills. That was a key skill if they were to be effective change agents.

The graduate assistants needed to constantly remember that they represented their profession. The data their evaluations generate is what they are to report. The opinions others may have about a child's capabilities are just that, opinions. An important role of mine supporting the graduate assistants was to assist them in resisting any possible pressure from educators, parents, authority figures or politicians to compromise the collected data. Above all, the graduate assistants had to avoid being drawn into the "politics" within a school, a school system or the system's community. Local politics in rural communities have years of historical development behind them. The graduate assistants do not have the time to invest to bring about a clear understanding of them. Their only role is to provide quality professional services with integrity to the data their training has enabled them to develop.

It was clear that the cooperative needed to develop an in-service training program for all the educators in the seven-member school systems that would make them knowledgeable in the new special education law so that they would be able to fully implement the law during the second school year. As stated earlier, this first school year was to establish a system of identifying the children with special needs and to begin the process of delivering services to those children. In the first year the disabilities of some children were severe enough to cause a delay in the implementation of their intervention programs. However, full implementation of all intervention plans was to be taking place by that second year. When I brought up the need for in-service training across the school systems to the co-op's executive director and the board of directors, they considered the answer to be obvious.

The graduate assistants and I were to do the training. After discussing the many demands on the graduate assistants' time, the board of directors authorized me to employ a professional educator to be primarily responsible for conducting the bulk of the in-service activities. However, that decision did not relieve me or the graduate assistants of the responsibility to conduct in-services within the school systems as local administrators determined the need for them. Fortunately, by the middle of the school year we had found a highly skilled educator to fulfill that role. She was so well respected that after several years with the cooperative, the Maryville City School System employed her as the director of their special education department.

On top of the obvious tasks that needed to be accomplished was the imperative to establish the trust of the seven-member school systems in the ability of the cooperative to deliver effective services to their schools in a totally fair and just manner. Through Bill Oakes and in some of the early meetings with member systems' school administrators, it became clear that the systems did not trust one another. They expected some of the member systems to try to use the cooperative to exploit their school system's resources. A few years later, I learned that this was a major issue with many of the newly created educational cooperatives across the state. This problem will be more thoroughly explained as well as the consequences the issue produced later.

Finding the trained individuals to employ for the school psychological assessments specialists positions was probably the easiest part of my new position. As explained earlier, I was quite familiar with the graduate students in the University of Tennessee school psychology program. None of the doctoral students had worked as a master's level school psychologist. My two years in that role in the Pinellas County Schools provided me with insights into the delivery of school psychological services that none of the other graduate students had, nor did most of the university faculty. The final year of graduate school found me delivering twenty hours a week of psychological service to Knoxville City Schools as a graduate assistant.

Since I met the state's qualifications as a certified school psychologist, the school system considered me to be a part-time school psychologist and assigned me comparable tasks. As a result, I had a solid background in delivering school psychological services and understood the delivery model Tennessee's larger cities were using. Pairing those experiences with my two years at the army's Psychological Warfare School provided me with insights that not only accelerated my completion of the requirements to graduate but provided me with insights I applied to the selection of the cooperative's graduate assistants. It was a given that the doctoral students were intelligent. They all possessed a high degree of dedication to making the world a better place and were willing to work hard towards that end.

In essence, the graduate assistants would be working as master's level school psychologists as I had done in St. Petersburg and Knoxville. They were entering a high-stress work environment where they had to function as change agents while delivering psychological services. As was the case with Army personnel assisting citizens from different cultures, the change agents had to have great respect for the cultural values of the communities in which they were working.

While respecting the local culture's ways of doing things, the change agents would have to assist the people to adjust and implement new behaviors in order for them to successfully accomplish their goals. For the change agent to be successful, he or she could not be pursuing the goal of becoming the "hero" to those they would be assisting. Being the "hero" means that those you have assisted have become dependent upon your leading them to their successes. When the hero of the story leaves the community, the community cannot maintain that success. They have lost their leader.

The vast majority of the graduate students were not from Tennessee. They did not expect to be employed as doctoral school psychologists in the state. Once their graduate school requirements were met and they received their doctorate degree, they would most likely not remain in East Tennessee, just as the Army's change agents were not going to be a permanent part of the communities in which they were working. The cooperative needed school psychology change agents who were going to assist their school systems to learn to meet the needs of their students in compliance with the new special education laws so thoroughly that the school system personnel would maintain that compliance without the change agent's presence.

I would need to ensure that the graduate assistants knew the special education laws thoroughly, were kept up to date on legal decisions concerning challenges to the law and challenges to the school systems in successfully meeting the requirements of the law. I also needed constantly to be implementing strategies to assist the change agents in reducing their sense of personal stress. Being the change agent is like trying to swim upstream against the current. You have to swim a lot harder to overcome the resistance of the current than would be the case going downstream. So it is with the social change agent. You are having to move against the resistance to change, which is much harder than just going along with, "Well, this is the way we have always done it."

Humor in its various forms has always been my way of

counteracting stress. I planned to interject as much of that as I could in working with the graduate assistants. Fortunately, all of the graduate students had experienced my attempts at humor during the two years we had been together. They had often participated in my humorous behaviors. I knew that it was important for all of us to maintain a good emotional support system for one another. Regardless of how strong we were emotionally, every one of us would become depressed. The resistance to major change was almost always intense. Our goal was to help the school systems to help their children. That goal was worthy of our being impatiently patient. We had to help each other if we were to be successful, if our schools, our teachers, our children were going to be successful. The goal was worthy of our patient persistence.

SEVEN
THE FIRST IN-SERVICES

At the end of July and into early August of 1973, I was busy planning my presentation to the teaching staff within each of the seven-member school systems. I was told that none of the teachers had been made aware that they would be implementing the new state special education law. My presentations would constitute the first time that they would learn what a dramatic impact the law would have on their work. I needed to do a good job.

As I had mentioned earlier, I had thoroughly studied the law and was exhilarated to be informing the teachers about these new resources available for their failing students. Based upon my two years as a school psychologist in the inner-city schools of St. Petersburg, Florida, and my experiences last year as a school psychologist/graduate assistant in the Knoxville City School System, I knew that it was highly likely that all the teachers had several disabled students in their classrooms. Those children were the ones who were failing while their teachers struggled to find educational strategies to help them with little or no success. Up to this school year, resources were lacking to engage school psychologists and other professionals to evaluate and identify children who had disabilities that qualified them for receiving special assistance. For children with appropriately identified disabilities, the school system would receive additional funding from the state to pay for those extra services. If the special services the disabled child needed could be provided in the regular classroom by a specialist, then they would be. If the special services could be implemented by the classroom teacher with consultation from various specialists, then the consultation would be provided.

I was so pleased to be the one to give the teachers this good news! At last, they would be getting additional assistance for those children floundering educationally in their classes! Up to this point special education was for only those children whom anyone could look at and say, "He needs to go to some special education center and get some help." Then the child would disappear. That child would never be in a regular public-school building. Now, for the first time, the teachers would have someone trained in school psychology, trained in the state-of-the-art evaluations of children with the kinds of disabilities a layperson would not recognize. How happy these educators were going to be that they would be getting the help they had been requesting for years!

Of course, I would have to be careful in my presentation to point out that there were changes in how the teachers would have to respond to the children's unique special needs, but that's where the school psychological services would be most helpful to them. Within the service providers' psycho-educational evaluations would be recommendations as to strategies that the teacher could implement in an attempt to improve the child's learning. The psychological service provider would also be available for direct consultations if a teacher requested it. Naturally, the teacher would need to keep data to determine if those strategies were actually helping the child. If the child was not progressing, the service provider would work with the teacher to make adjustments. The child's parents would be involved in the planning, evaluating, and adjusting process for the child. Other relevant professionals could also be involved.

Because of this new law that I would explain in my presentations, the teachers were finally getting help. The teacher at last would have a support system in her search for a way to make a true difference in the life of a child. Who in education wouldn't be gratified by this change in Tennessee's educational model? While it was true that during this first year of funding the law there was no money for an increase in special education teachers or other direct service providers, that kind of funding would come the following year. This first year was for major increases in evaluating and identifying children with disabilities that significantly interfered with the normal educational experience offered to all children.

As noted earlier, in that sense, the special education law is a civil rights law. All children have the right to an equal opportunity for an education. Only when a child has an identified disability that is clearly interfering with the child's ability to benefit from the regular educational process are educators allowed to treat that child differently in school. In essence, the special education law allows the school system not to treat the disabled child like all the other children. This is a serious legal matter. The law requires procedural safeguards so that those aspects of the child's educational life that can be dealt with in a normal manner will be.

The special education law contains many directives on how to maintain records to ensure the child receives an appropriate education both in the area of his special needs and in those areas that require that he be treated like any other child in the school system. The directives and subsequent paperwork appeared to me to be very logical. In fact, maintaining the child's educational records as required made whatever adjustments the teacher had to make with the child more manageable than simply trying to help the child without a carefully developed plan and monitoring system.

I did realize that the number of school psychology doctoral students working in the schools was not great enough to meet the needs once the teachers began realizing how many children they had who probably had qualifying disabilities. Still, the ratio of students to school psychology service providers was lower than it had been for me when I worked in the St. Petersburg or Knoxville schools. I couldn't do anything about the lack of adequate funding the state was providing other than to acknowledge that it wasn't enough.

Taking a deep breath, I entered the crowded cafeteria of the high school. It was packed with teachers and staff from all four of the schools in this system. The air was buzzing with small group conversations as people were asking each other how their summer vacations had been. The teachers were eager to get started. They had classrooms to make ready for the arrival of the children, lesson plans to finish, scheduling of special events to prepare for and a host of other tasks to perform that these group meetings were preventing them from accomplishing. My presentation was the first big event of their three days of meetings that began their school year. Energy was in the air.

Polite applause followed my introduction to them. My presentation started with how pleased I was to be the one to share with them that the special education law newly passed by the Tennessee state legislature was finally providing them with assistance for the evaluation of their poor learners to determine if they had a disability that fit the state's criteria of disability. If a child was found to have a qualifying disability, the next step was to determine if that disability was interfering with the child's learning. Assuming that a child had a disability, and that disability was negatively affecting his learning, a plan needed to be developed that remediated the teaching/learning effort. The school psychology doctoral student could provide assistance in planning how to adjust the classroom instruction to most benefit the child without overburdening the classroom teacher. If the disabling condition required some educational services to be provided outside of the classroom, plans would be developed to accommodate those needs.

My comments were met with glassy-eyed stares and silence, total silence. I thought there would be lots of smiles and nodding of heads.

I was wrong. While I was unsure of the meaning of their non-verbal feedback, I realized that I was not a big hit.

Then my presentation went into how the law mandated that records be kept documenting the evaluation process; then, the group determination process that decided if a child's disability was interfering with his learning and, if so, what was going to be done to change that; and, finally, evaluating the child on at least a quarterly basis to determine if the intervention plan was working. If it wasn't working, the plan needed to be changed. Of course, the child's parents had to be involved and approve of all of the decisions.

That last part brought people to their feet. They were shaking their fists at me while shouting statements such as the following: "You are destroying American education!" "Who are you to tell us what to do?" "You're a fool!" "No one can do all that for one child and teach a classroom of NORMIES!" "Where are we going to find the time to do all of this and teach our children?"

The high school principal escorted me to my car. I had two more presentations to make that day. Fortunately, that first school system had the most overtly negative responses to what I had to share.

I want to remind you that this was August 1973. The first school system I was in has changed dramatically over the years. It has been a leader in integrating services with special needs children, culturally diverse children and parent involvement. Almost always, when there is a change in the school system's superintendent/director of schools, or school board members, or state governor, or president of the country there are significant changes in a school system. Various reports indicate that over the last decade or so, the average superintendent remains in office somewhere between five and seven years. It sometimes appears to be a truism that if you are running for a political office you have to have a position on how to improve education. In short, it is unlikely that a school system in 2030 will be a mirror image of its 1973 self.

My concept as to how the new special education law was going to be received needed adjustment. It was clear that I had to prepare the doctoral students for the negative responses they might be encountering as they performed their psycho-educational assessments. The graduate students had to know and fully understand the law before they stepped into a school. They needed to understand the fear the teachers felt and why they felt it. These doctoral students were the change agents. Introducing these new procedures to educators would be similar to my Army work at the Special Warfare Center. The doctoral students needed to be trained as if they were part of a special warfare team entering isolated communities with the mission of assisting the local population to utilize the new resources being made available to them. Above all else, doctoral students needed to know how important it was that they value the educators they worked with. It was absolutely essential that they value even those educators who strongly disagreed with them on how to serve a special needs child.

To my way of thinking, we were assaulting the belief systems of many of those educators opposing the concepts of the special education law. Their concept of the classroom teacher's role was that they were to teach those children who were functioning at grade level, were ready to learn the lessons to be presented and at the rate they were presented. If a child could not do that, the child was to be removed from the class and fixed. Not only was the learning problem to be fixed, but when he returned to the classroom, he was caught up on the lessons he had missed, enabling him to be ready to receive the lesson for that day. The special education law did not support this belief system. Changing someone's core belief system is hard for that individual and very hard for the change agent to accomplish.

Many teachers were pleased that the special education law was now a reality. They wanted to assist all children and were deeply frustrated that, until now, they had no way of getting significant professional support to do what needed to be done. They had the desire to do what needed to be done. Their blocking factors included the lack of extra time to accomplish the new paperwork required to document their efforts, their successes and to make adjustment when necessary. In addition, they had the fear of being brought into a due process hearing by some angry parent and trying to defend themselves in that setting. The list goes on. In short, the desire to serve was there. Finding the time or getting the support needed to accomplish the tasks was in question.

There was much to do to prepare the graduate students before they entered their first school buildings. I knew that we could do it. I had participated in Army training exercises out of Fort Bragg, North Carolina. Several times a year the Army trainees went into the rural mountain communities of North Carolina to practice what we instructors had taught in war games with Special Forces trainees. I would be doing the same basic training with the graduate students in rural communities on the other side of the mountains, the Tennessee side.

As for the doctoral students, fortunately, I knew all of them. I had been studying with them for the past two years. I knew their strengths, their determination to be successful and their overwhelming desire to help children. There was an added bonus. They were really smart.

It wasn't until well into August that Bill discovered that the cooperative was not going to receive the designated special education funds for the psychological services from the state on a monthly basis. The state had informed him and the superintendents that the special education funds were to be released on a reimbursement basis at the end of each quarter of the year. The first quarter of the year included July, August and September.

The cooperative did not have the funds to pay the graduate assistants their first paychecks at the end of August. They would receive their first paycheck at the end of September or in early October. I spent a lot of time on the telephone explaining to bank officials and creditors why many of the graduate students could not make their payments on time. I requested that they not be penalized for their late payments. To the best of my knowledge, none of the graduate students were assigned extra fees for their late payments.

EIGHT
STRESS AND ITS RELEASE

As stated earlier, we knew that introducing major changes for the seven-member school systems of the educational cooperative was going to be stressful for both the school system educators and the cooperative's change agents. The changes the systems would have to make in implementing Tennessee's 1973 new special education laws were massive. In turn, the role of psychological services was critical in ensuring the systems' success.

Again, the first year's extra funding was for psych services to identify the children who met the state's criteria for having specific, defined disabilities that interfered with their experiencing the benefits the regular educational program offered to non-disabled children. Once the qualified disabled children were identified, psych services would play a key role in designing and implementing an individualized educational plan for each of those children. As the intervention plans were being implemented, the systems would systematically evaluate the effectiveness of the educational adjustments periodically throughout the school year. That first few years of implementing the law, more students suspected of having a learning disability were referred for evaluation than for any other category. Prior to passage of the law, many school systems had never considered having a learning disability to be a significant factor in student failure. Adjustments made within the regular classroom environment could remove blocking variables for many of the students with this category of disability. The child's multidisciplinary team (M-Team) of educators and the child's parents would make their recommendations and they would quickly go into effect.

The 1974-1975 school year was also the year that the federal special education law came into the picture. That law was nearly identical to Tennessee's special education law. One big difference was that the Tennessee law included the category of "gifted" as a condition that could require appropriate educational adjustments if certain criteria were met. The federal law did not address the issue of giftedness. The federal law provided federal funds to the state of Tennessee to enable its school systems to meet the federal requirements for that first year and for following years with the amount of funding to ultimately increase to cover forty percent of the total cost in meeting the obligations of the law.

It needs to be remembered that the federal government considered the state governments to be in charge of educating their children. When federal officials went into a school system to evaluate the delivery of services to special needs children, they were investigating how the state caused that school system to meet the requirement of the law. They were not, on paper, evaluating a local school system's delivery model. On the surface, this appears to be a minor point. However, in some circumstances in court cases, this point was an important one.

For the cooperative's school systems, the 1973-1974 school year also meant creating a new evaluation process using school psychological services on a systematic basis for the first time in their history. This was also the first time that the seven school systems had ever been a member of an educational cooperative or shared service providers across their boundaries on such a large scale. It was also the first time that all those providing school psychological services had ever delivered them to school systems with the exception of myself as the director of those services.

The issues that the senior graduate students in school psychology faced as graduate assistants delivering their professional services to the co-op's school systems were gigantic. Naturally, they had doubts concerning their ability to properly perform the duties expected of a school psychologist. However, the special situations they were about to encounter were clearly unusual. The educators they were to work with did not understand what the special education law required of them, had never encountered the massive educational changes they were going to have to make to meet the requirements of the law, disagreed with those requirements as they learned about them, lacked the training needed to make the changes, did not understand what school psychology services were, had no idea as to what the educational cooperative was and did not trust the motivations of the cooperative's other member school systems. Perhaps the most disturbing issue the graduate assistants would have to face was the stark reality that the state had not made available to the school systems the funds to employ enough school psychology providers to accomplish all of the evaluations, consultations, parent/teacher meetings, report writing and re-evaluations required of the service.

There was no doubt in my mind that the graduate assistants were going to be successful. After all, most if not all of them were entering their third or fourth year of graduate school. At this stage of their doctoral programs, they had completed the vast majority of their required coursework and were focusing on preparing for comprehensive departmental exams and developing their dissertation research projects.

Despite the professional training that far exceeded the key issues of the state's requirements to be certified as master's level school psychologists, I knew that the stresses placed upon these doctoral students were going to be high. The cooperative was going to have to develop stress-reducing strategies for the staff on a systematic basis. My first priority was to support them. Whenever any staff person requested a one-on-one meeting to discuss a situation in the schools, I would schedule the meeting as soon as possible. That meeting was a priority.

As approved by the co-op's board of directors, the job description for all graduate students included being paid for attendance at the Friday afternoon staff meetings and being provided with release time to attend at least one major professional conference a year. The agenda for the staff meetings included discussing any cases concerning the evaluation of a child, the support provided through the schools in meeting a child's needs, difficulties in working with personalities within the school setting and a host of other issues that the staff needed to problem-solve with the group.

Developing the group support system was an important aspect in coping with the stress of the work environment. No one was expected to know how to address or solve all of the problems we would encounter. We had to tap into the collective wisdom of the group. The group had a massive amount of knowledge and problem-solving skills. Each one of them was highly intelligent intellectually, socially and emotionally. As mentioned, they all had been extremely well trained in the state-of-the-art skills necessary to be functioning school psychologists. All of them thoroughly understood that they were going to be a key force in furthering the development of educational services to children with and without disabilities. They had a solid understanding of the role of a change agent. In addition, they had already become their collective emotional support group during their joint experiences of being graduate students together.

The wide diversity of backgrounds the individuals brought to the group prior to their graduate school days enhanced the creative problem-solving capabilities we could all draw upon for support. Among the group were three military veterans, a few former schoolteachers, some former mental health service providers and others with equally valuable cultural experiences.

Using humor to reduce stress was a natural response for me. I had used it while in the Army and while working in the inner-city schools of St. Petersburg and the city schools of Knoxville, as well as during my two years at the university. During those years at the university some of my funny stunts had reached the level of being told so many times that their relation to the truth had become rather thin. Our new staff of graduate assistants anticipated that we would find and share a humorous perspective for our efforts in assisting children and teachers.

Those early days of the cooperative found that the stress-reducing displays of humor were most apparent during the Friday afternoon staff meetings but not limited to that setting. Shortly after the graduate assistants or I had conducted the preschool in-services in all of our schools and were encountering a great deal of hostility from angry, frightened and confused teachers, we began our Friday afternoon staff meetings.

The psychological and special education services offices were in a big classroom of an old school building. The school building had a hallway that led to an entrance to a relatively modern high school. The classroom was huge. It had a large walk-in cloak closet much like my first and second grade classrooms in Granite City, Illinois, back in 1948. That closet was where all of us children hung our coats and left our bulky galoshes on rainy days. The cooperative's staff's cloakroom had a "hangy-down light bulb" with a long string attached to be pulled when you wanted the light on. The ceilings inside the closet and the classroom were unusually high. I wouldn't have been surprised if the building maintenance crew had told me that there were at least sixteen feet between the floors and the ceilings.

Standard school building folding tables were placed in a square arrangement in this ancient classroom so that all of the staff could face each other during the staff meetings. During the meetings, incident after incident was presented of angry encounters the staff had had with various educators in their schools. I tried to calm the practitioners with explanatory comments to help them understand that the teachers were not angry with them as specific individuals. They were angry at the lack of preparedness their administrators had provided before they were expected to implement the new system. They were afraid that they could not maintain their current level of professional teaching while trying to implement new teaching strategies they did not know if they knew how to do. My words didn't relieve the staff's need to vent their frustrations.

During one of those early staff meetings our first opportunity to share in-group humor presented itself. As various staff members were interrupting each other trying to express their dismay at the anger they encountered, something hit me on the side of my head. It was a paper wad. Looking in the direction that it had come from, I saw Frank, the former combat marine, grinning at me as he wadded up another piece of paper to be sent my way. Quickly, I smiled back and ducked as the paper wad flew over the top of my head. As if I were throwing a grenade, I lobbed a ball of paper accurately at Frank's head. Looking up from his task of creating a new pile of ammo, he shouted, "In-coming!"

This was war. Frank immediately tipped his table over as he hunched down behind it to launch his missiles as if they were mortar rounds. Instinctively responding, my table tipped to the floor. One of the other graduate assistants pushed a pile of ammo he had been making my way. The extra ammo allowed me to return fire.

Bam, bam, all of the other tables slammed to the floor to be used as protection from the paper wads coming from all directions. All of us were engaged in this battle. There were no sides. You just fired your paper wads at any and all targets. We laughed and howled until we nearly ran out of notebook paper.

Once the tables were returned to their proper positions and we had collectively picked up most of the spent brass and ammo, we returned to our staff meeting agenda. The tension was gone. Collectively, we were supportive of the frustrations experienced by each of us, sympathetic to the needs of the educators to express their stress, and able to share insights on positive strategies for assisting teachers in addressing their concerns.

At a later staff meeting, but still in the early part of the school year, Doug, a near all-but-dissertation graduate assistant, related this story. His rural school system had not assigned a school administrator to be the director of special education services. When he tried to establish to whom he should report about special education issues, he was passed from one administrator to another. None of them had an interest in acquiring information about the special education law or in telling anyone else what to do regarding it. More often than not, Doug was the person people in the system went to when they had a special education issue to resolve and to obtain explanatory information about it. Fortunately, Doug and all the other graduate assistants knew the law quite well. We were constantly covering it during staff meetings and staff training times.

After a few weeks had passed, Mr. Green (a pseudonym), the school bus coordinator and custodian of all of the system's textbooks seemed to be the one administrator that Doug could persuade to make some decisions or to provide Doug with some positive direction for getting something done. Mr. Green was long in years within the system. Everyone knew him and he seemed to know everyone. He constantly held the stub of a cigar in his hand. Most of the time it was not lit, but he would frequently move it to his mouth and suck on it as if he were really smoking it. Mr. Green had a particular fondness for one phrase that seemed to be used often with Doug or anyone else. That phrase would be followed by the name of the person Mr. Green was speaking to. With this information concerning Mr. Green, you can more readily appreciate the story Doug told at a staff meeting concerning his seeking information from this supervisor.

Doug's telling of the story went something like this, "Well, I couldn't find any records of past psychological reports on children in the system. I went to the trailer/temp building Mr. Green was in. He was there. His desk sat in the middle of rows of shelves stacked full of textbooks.

"Taking his cigar out of his mouth and holding it suspended in front of his face, he gives me his, 'Hello, Douglas' greeting. 'What do you need now?'

'I can't find any old records of psychological reports the system has on its kids. Do you know where they are?'

'Good, Douglas. That's good. Yeah, that's good,' he says with a big grin and puts the cigar back in his mouth.

'Do you know where they are?' I asked him again.

'Well, Douglas, why don't you go down there,' he says waving his arm down an aisle of book-crammed shelves and pointing with his stub of cigar, 'There's a cardboard box at the end that might have some of those.'

"Sure enough, there, on the floor, was a cardboard box full of file folders at the far end of the bookshelves. I picked up the first one from the file. It had some sort of psychological report dated 1945. The next one was dated in the early 1950's. There was no order to the time of the reports. They were just thrown into the box.

"Picking up a couple of the reports, I took them back to Mr. Green. 'Mr. Green, I found some in the box.'

"Taking the stubby cigar from his mouth and looking up at me, he said, 'Good. That's good. That's good, Douglas.'

'Is this it? Is this all there is?' I asked.

'You may have something there, Douglas. That's good. Yeah, that's good.'

'Ok, I'm going to start a whole new filing system for the schools on this.'

'Ahh, (puff, puff on that cigar butt), Yah, that's good. That's good, Douglas.' "

Doug looked at all of us in exasperation. I immediately pretended to take a cigar from my mouth and loudly stated, "That's good. Yeah, that's good, Douglas." My comments were echoed by several others as we all laughed together.

Mr. Green's words were often used to bring humor into stressful times at staff meetings and in other gathering places. Those words always brought warm smiles and knowing chuckles.

Our humor was spontaneous. Seldom did we plan to do or say something to make us all laugh or at least change our perspective. It just seemed to happen on its own, a product of the moment. For example, there had to have been some really frustrating account being told. Maybe it was about a school principal refusing to implement the recommendations of the professional members of the child's multidisciplinary team. At this point, let's speculate that their recommendations included allowing a teacher's aide trained in positive reinforcement to be in the regular classroom with a child diagnosed with an autistic disorder to assist him in maintaining focus on correctly completing his lessons as he manifested appropriate social behavior in that setting. It appeared that the resistance to the recommendations of the multidisciplinary team was a violation of special education law and destructive to the child. The issue before the provider of psychological services and the entire staff was what should be done to solve this problem. As the account of whatever problem was being told, anger was building and being expressed by the staff.

Without thinking, I became inspired to climb onto the tabletop, stomp across it and jump onto adjoining tables as I shouted in a loud, authoritarian voice trying to mimic a French accent and pretending to be Napoleon Bonaparte, "How dare the English stand in the way of our pursuit of injustice for all. Off with their heads, off with their heads, and may they always be used as bowling balls." Then I'd calmly sit back down in my chair and ask if anyone had a more positive way of helping the principal understand the needs of the child and why implementing the recommendations would be helpful to all concerned. Always after such a stunt as that and after the laughter had subsided, excellent ideas and suggestions would be articulated for resolving the conflicts.

During that first year, the Alcoa school system graciously

directed its maintenance staff to build shelves along all four sides of the large walk-in cloak closet of the psychology and special education services room. This allowed us to store in an easily accessible space various test kits, poster-making materials for in-services and other relevant materials that were frequently used by the staff. The shelves were about three feet deep and four feet high with five or six levels of shelving. The very top shelf was around three feet from the ceiling. I keep repeating that the walk-in closet was a large one. Even when all of the overhead lights in the classroom were on, the interior of that closet was black. It was not possible to recognize what test kit you were picking up from a shelf unless you pulled the white string hanging down for the one bare light bulb in the space.

Our host school system had also built us room divider structures that carved out an office area in which confidential discussions could be held and cubical-type spaces for the staff to use while leaving enough open space for staff meetings. The dividers were about three inches thick and made of a rigid, stringy-like substance that was cemented or glued together. The panels provided a solid wall that absorbed sound. This fabricated structure was stabilized by two-by-four braces at the floor level. The confidential office space panels were about twelve feet high. The sound-absorbing quality of those panels provided the privacy level needed by the staff and myself for various confidential discussions. Unless otherwise needed, that space served as my office. A large metal desk, file cabinet and two chairs fit nicely into the space. The cubicles used for general purposes had wall panels that were about six feet tall. The cost of the material played a role in determining their size. All of the cubical/office spaces had a desk, file cabinet and telephone.

On one occasion I decided to have some fun with staff members by climbing into the shelves to surprise the first person entering the walk-in closet/storage space. I cleared out a shelf that was a little above eye level and fully reclined on it, trying to mimic the image of a reclining Buddha I had seen in a *National Geographic* magazine.

When Barry walked in, pulled down on the "hangy-down" light

bulb string and discovered me in the prone position resting my head on my bent arm, he grinned at me and, in his typically calm voice, asked, "Jerry what are you doing there?"

In my best deep Buddha calming voice I replied, "I am the reclining Buddha."

That broke the calm within Barry. He began joyously laughing as I climbed down from the shelf. He helped me brush off the layers of dust I had accumulated waiting for someone to enter.

Another time I decided to climb up to the very top shelf and sat Buddha-style in the corner of it facing the door to the storage space. It was a harder climb than I had anticipated, but I got there. The space was cramped. I kept bumping my head on the ceiling. My vision of being discovered by the first staff person entering the cloak closet converted storage space was that as they looked up to grab the string that would turn on that lone light bulb, I would be discovered. We would both laugh, I would climb down, and we would be full of good cheer. That's not how it happened.

One of the graduate assistants briskly walked into the closet. She was intent on looking on the opposite side of the shelving where the intelligence test kits were stored. Without looking up she reached for and found that "hangie-down string" and turned the light bulb on.

She hadn't seen me. What should I do? As she reached for a test kit, I stated in my studied, quiet Buddha voice, "Not that one."

Her hand froze. She looked to the left. She looked to the right. She moved her hand two test kits over and began to pick that one up.

"Not that one either."

Once again, her hand froze. For a few seconds she just stood there with her hand suspended. Then calmly, quietly, she walked out of the room. Laughing, I called out to her as I started climbing down the shelf to ground level. We both had a good laugh at my attempts at humor and the confusion she experienced. Later she explained that she thought she was hearing the bleed-over from a speaker connected to the school system's high school sound system. The high school was connected to this older building by a closed hallway. The other end of the older building's hallway held the administrative offices of the school system. Once in a while you could hear bits of announcements over the high school's speakers at our end of the old building. Her reasoning was sound. We still got some nice chuckles over my attempt to spread joy.

At other times it would occur to me to surprise a graduate assistant who I thought would appreciate the humor of my hiding in the chair well of my desk as he entered the office space. When he entered, I would speak from my hiding spot by saying something like, "Hi, I'm Jerry's talking desk. You can talk to me. I know everything he does. All his files are in the desk drawers. I've held every one of them." This scene produced some highly creative and funny exchanges.

Not all of my behaviors and the staff's in sharing our laughter and valuing of each other occurred at the office. On one occasion, while driving towards Knoxville on a major four-lane highway, I realized I was catching up to John's car. John Adams was working with the cooperative as the director of an environmental grant the cooperative had from the U. S. Office of Education as he was completing his doctoral dissertation. I thought I would surprise him by tearing two eye-holes into a brown paper bag, putting the bag over my head and driving up beside him and turning my head to face him.

This was what the unknown comic wore when he appeared on "The Gong Show," a popular TV show at that time. The basic format of the program was to have "amateur" acts on the show and immediately evaluate the performance. If the act was particularly bad, the TV host, Chuck Barris, would hit a large gong in the middle of the singer's screeching song or the tuba player's tortured notes. Then he'd go on stage and pull the performer off with a large shepherd's type of hook. Clearly, the show employed actors to be very bad in whatever they did. Sometimes the performance was excellent, which caused the audience be in suspense as to the quality of the next act.

Between performances the unknown comic would appear with a

brown paper bag over his head and look into the camera through his two eyeholes while proceeding to tell dumb jokes that accompanied his strange arm and leg movements. Those movements were supposed to be complicated dance moves. Naturally, the gong would ring and the unknown comic would be dragged off. The very bizarreness of the show produced laughs. The one constant of it was the unexpected appearance of the unknown comic. Somehow that show and the TV show titled "Laugh-In," were often topics of conversation among the cooperative's school psychology providers.

So, back to my pretending to be the "Unknown Comic." It took all of my attention to keep the car centered in the fast lane of the four-lane highway while picking up an old brown paper bag off the floor of the passenger side of the car, tearing eye holes in it and then placing it over my head while maintaining a steady rate of speed. With all of that going on, I didn't dare try to determine if John knew I was approaching him on the fast-lane side. Fortunately, my car and John's car were the only two within close distance on this section of the road, or I wouldn't have been able to attempt to pull this off.

At last, the paper bag was on my head, and I had enough vision out of the torn eye sockets to maneuver the car beside John's. I looked over to see John in his driver's seat just as he looked over at me. Both of us had brown paper bags over our heads. We were twins. We were the Unknown Comic twins. Neither one of us had realized that the other one was preparing to surprise the other with this stunt. Naturally, we shared this story at staff meetings and in other social gatherings. It's been retold many times. Just a few months ago John and I shared it with Barry once again.

Every few months or so we would have staff social meetings some Saturday afternoon and at other convenient times. We enjoyed holidays at staff meetings. Just before Christmas break, we would dedicate a Friday afternoon to a visit from Santa. That was me in costume distributing humorous gifts. The event would go something like this: Santa would start complaining about the poor performance of his new elves and then give someone a rusty lunch box. When the receiver of it opened the box, it contained an old banana peel. Santa used that as proof of the poor performance of his new staff. At the end of the school year, the staff often went somewhere for a group adventure on a weekend. I remember a group of us canoeing to a mountain stream for the purpose of swimming in one of its upstream pools. Another year we went to a camp near a ruby mine and joined in that activity.

NINE
BEGINNING TO LEARN THE CULTURE

As with all communities, to those living in them their established cultural norms are simply the way things are. They are the normal way of doing things and do not need explaining. It's in other places, like Duluth, Minnesota, that people need to explain why they do what they do in such a different manner. My experience of moving from place to place as a child and into my adult years had sensitized me to this attitude. I can remember the many taverns that our family frequented in Wisconsin. The local tavern was and still is a welcoming community gathering point for many.

However, that is not the case in most taverns in the South. It still is a rare sight to see adults bring children into a bar in rural areas of Tennessee. When I first began working on a dredge boat off the Texas coast, the common response to the inquiring question, "How are you?" was "Mighty fine!" I never heard that response in any other community. An identifying response of someone who has spent a lot of time in Cincinnati, Ohio, who did not completely hear everything you had said, is "Please?" whereas in other communities you may hear the request to repeat what was said as "Pardon?" "I'm sorry?" or

"Excuse me?" A quick way to identify someone who has lived in East Tennessee for a while is the colloquial phrase used when leaving someone's company, "See ya."

The local norms of speaking and behaving are so ingrained within their communities that those using them are usually unaware that they have become accepted as normal behavior. Those behaviors are so common that anyone not following them is easily identified as an outsider, not one of us. A "not one of us" person is often suspect. That individual, "someone not from around here," must earn the native's trust before they can be totally accepted into the "real" community. It seems to me that the more isolated a community, the more ingrained are the unconsciously accepted cultural norms of that community.

It was important to the success of the educational cooperative's mission of assisting its East Tennessee school systems in developing educational services for their special needs children that the cooperative's employees understand the regional norms as quickly as possible. Since the vast majority of the co-op's staff in those early years were doctoral graduate students who had grown up in other parts of the country, there was a potential problem. They could be perceived as "those outsiders coming in and telling us what to do."

The school systems had good reason to suspect those from other states wanting to work in their schools. Remember, we are talking about 1973. The American culture as a whole was different than it is today. A comment made to me by the Monroe County superintendent as he explained the difficulty of finding qualified teacher applicants serves as an example. "Oh, sure," he said, "we receive lots of teaching applications from people from up North. I've got one that came in the mail yesterday. This young woman has just gotten her teacher's certification from a university in New York. She stated that she would be a perfect teacher for our children because she understands the Southern culture. She has been taking banjo lessons so she would be a perfect fit for our system." He went on to explain that he has dozens of similar applications. What he needs are applications from teachers who are from the region. "They don't have to be taught to unlearn cultural stereotypes about our children or us." I understood his point of view.

My problem was that I was also an outsider. My saving grace was that I knew some of the regional cultural issues although certainly not all of them. Above all else, I knew that this region had just as many gifted educators, quick learners and caring people as any other region of the country. Their unique cultural differences were to be valued just as was the case for those of large city schools, Gulf Coast schools and all the other school systems across the country.

Having had experiences in various parts of the South, I had perceived a sense of resentment against northerners. So many "Yankees" seemed to assume that they were superior to "those poverty-driven, under-educated Southerners." As an automatic defense mechanism to this biased perception held by some Northerners, many Southerners prefaced their statements with something to the effect that, "Well, you probably know more about this than I do, but..." I have heard Southerners with doctorate degrees who are experts on the topic they are about to comment on begin their statements in this manner. It's not that they think that those being addressed know more about the topic than they do. It's a test of the person they are addressing. If that person seems to agree that he knows more about the topic than the speaker, then the speaker knows he is speaking to someone who thinks he is better than the speaker. That person may now be considered an "arrogant fool." If the outsider wants to be valued and accepted by someone within the community, he must not be condescending. He must value the other as an equal.

You may recall reading the earlier story concerning my being interviewed by the cooperative's board of directors for my employment with them. One board member was dressed as if he had just gotten off his tractor to attend the meeting. Late in the interview process he asked me what I knew about the university's verbal tonal method of teaching. Fortunately, I knew something about this new method of assisting children with serious hearing problems. One of the main researchers of that method was a friend of mine. I also knew that I was being tested. I responded to the question by explaining a few of the basic principles of the approach as I understood them and concluded by stating, "I suspect that you may have a more extensive understanding than I do."

He responded by stating he had a grandchild in that program at the university. Then he went into great detail describing the verbal tonal method, the research data verifying the effectiveness of the program and his hope that the cooperative would sponsor such a program among its member school systems.

I had passed the test. It was important that I make sure that the graduate students could pass similar tests. Equally important was the awareness that we would all share the new lessons we would learn concerning our adopted culture. This would be essential for all of us to be as successful as possible.

In the spring of that first year, another opportunity was presented me in learning about the cooperative's school systems and their culture. A supervisor in the Maryville City School System asked me what I thought about the educators in the county. Immediately, I sensed that I was being tested. This supervisor was highly valued within his school system and across the region. I respected and liked him as well. His school system was one of three school systems in Blount County. There was another city system, Alcoa, and the county had its own school system. All three systems operated independently of the others. A high level of competition existed between the school systems.

My response was something like, "Some truly outstanding educators teach here. They would be outstanding in any school system in the country. This region is fortunate to have them in their schools. In your system a high school English teacher, Ms. Brown, simply inspires her students with her love of literature. She brings the books alive for her students. They want to read and discuss them. On top of that she has developed some excellent strategies for working with her disabled students. In the other city system, there is a guidance counselor, Ms. Washington, who is gifted in understanding adolescents. She has started a student support group with a waiting list of young people wanting to join. At this point she is considering developing several student support groups. In the county school system an elementary school teacher, Ms. White, is teaching math through rhymes and songs. The children love learning that way and seem to be learning much more rapidly than those taught in the traditional manner."

"Well," said the supervisor with a generous smile, "Without knowing it you have paid me the highest compliment. The English teacher is my sister. The math teacher is my sister-in-law, and the guidance counselor is one of my best friends."

It is important to note that my praise of those educators was heartfelt. I really was impressed with their skills. A few years later we helped a group of these excellent educators to write down some of their classroom strategies for reaching students. The cooperative published their collection in a book titled, *What's Cooking in the Classroom*.

Yes, in small rural communities, it seems as if everyone is connected. To be critical of one person is to be critical of many relatives and friends who support that one person. You simply don't want to do that unless you have an important, pressing reason for doing so. The negative statement has to be focused on the misunderstanding the person has of the situation rather than the character of the individual in question. The misunderstanding can be corrected. The personality of the individual is another issue.

The county supervisor's words of "Good, Douglas. Yes, that's good," while pantomiming puffing on a stubby cigar were often used to bring humor into stressful times at staff meetings and in other gathering places. Those words always brought warm smiles and knowing chuckles. Mr. Green was a good man with a dry sense of humor. At that time, we were all unaware of his long history in that system. For example, we were ignorant of the fact that he had been a political rival of the current superintendent. As that school year was coming to a close, I did not know if Mr. Green's school system would continue to receive school psychological services from the cooperative or if it would even remain a member of the cooperative. I did know that the system needed someone to be in charge of the special education program. Over the course of the year, Mr. Green had become the one administrator within the system that more and more educators turned to for guidance in implementing the law. On several occasions I had discussed this need with Mr. Green. He agreed that the system needed such a supervisor. Unfortunately, he did not want to be that person.

Together, we explored the possibility of other supervisors taking on the role. We both acknowledged that none of them seemed to fit what was needed. Doug, the graduate assistant serving that system, spent a lot of time talking to Mr. Green about taking the position in the hopes that the superintendent would decide to fund it for the coming year. At last, Mr. Green agreed to accept the position on a half-time basis if that was what the superintendent and school board wanted.

By the middle of July, the superintendent had decided to bring the issue of employing someone on a part-time basis to be the supervisor of special education up for a vote by the system's school board. They would also decide if the system would remain a member of the cooperative and continue to contract for school psychological services through it. The school board meeting was scheduled to begin at 7:00 PM in the gymnasium of the system's one high school. I was invited to address the school board about the need for a supervisor of special education and explain to the board why I thought continuing to receive psychological services through the cooperative would be in their best interest.

I did not know what to expect as I prepared for that evening meeting. It was unusually hot even for the middle of July. It would not be appropriate to wear a coat and tie. I would be covered in sweat before the meeting began. A short-sleeved white shirt with a tie was as formal as I could afford to be. I assumed that the superintendent and all the school board members would be wearing about the same "uniforms." Another assumption I made was that most, if not all, of the school board members would not know much about the special education laws. I would have to provide them with a global understanding of it so that they would realize the importance of having tight administrative supervision of the system's special education activities. The system was currently at grave risk of unwittingly committing serious violations of the law. That would put it at risk of being placed under sanctions from the state and federal departments of education. In turn, the system would probably be facing multiple lawsuits from parents of children with disabilities. They would lose in almost every case. I also knew that there was not a way that the system could obtain the high quality of school psychological services they were receiving from the cooperative for anywhere near the amount of funds they were providing the co-op. My goals were clear.

First, I was to educate them about the law and their need for someone within the system to be in charge of fulfilling the law's requirements. Secondly, I needed to educate the board about how the cooperative delivered school psychological services within their system and why it was in their best interest to continue that service. Since the system's superintendent had never attended a cooperative board of directors meeting during my tenure with the cooperative, I was not sure that he fully understood the law.

From home, it took more than an hour to drive to the meeting's location. That July evening was really hot. Just walking from the parking lot to the gym building brought a haze of sweat to my face. I was not sure about what to expect when I arrived. Whatever I expected was not what opened up before me. At the far end of the building, at the end of the basketball court, was a large teacher's desk with the superintendent seated behind it. His outstretched and crossed legs rested on the top of the desk. He was casually talking to a couple of men sitting to the side of the desk in a line of twelve chairs or so pushed back against the far wall. In front of the desk were five short rows of the same type of folding chairs as those lined up against the wall.

Even though the outside doors to the gym were open, the temperature inside the building was greater than the hot outside air. In short, it was really hot. Without moving from his seated position, the superintendent waved to me to approach him. He greeted me and motioned to the three or four men in the line of the chairs against the wall as he introduced me to the school board members. He noted that when all of the school board members had taken their seats, the meeting would begin. They would need to address several agenda items before my presentation, he stated. Until then, I was to take a seat in one of the chairs on the basketball court placed in front of his desk. None of the board members or the superintendent wore a necktie. I was overdressed.

After twenty minutes or so, all of the school board members were seated in the line of chairs pressed against the wall. A few other people arrived to sit in the many unfilled chairs surrounding me. I assumed they were interested in issues about to be discussed by the board. The items discussed before I was called were tedious and boring. The superintendent brought them up. He told the board what he thought they ought to do and asked if there were any questions. There were none. Someone made a motion to do what the superintendent recommended. The motion was seconded and passed. The whole process took place in a quiet, casual manner. The superintendent never removed his feet from the desktop.

Finally, I was called forward to speak to the board. The superintendent introduced me as Dr. Morton from the cooperative and the director of its psychological and special education services. He explained that I wanted to talk to the board about the need for the system to have a halftime director of special education services as well as their continuing to be a member of the cooperative. In turn, they would continue to receive the school psychology and in-service components provided by it.

I began explaining the many requirements the law contained in evaluating, serving and monitoring the progress of the children who met the qualifications as special needs children requiring specialized services from the school system. After thoroughly covering the legal liabilities to the school system if it failed to carry out the mandates of the law, I realized that these explanations had taken up a lot of time. Many board members seemed uninterested in what I was saying. Several of them seemed more interested in wiping sweat from their faces than understanding the importance of my words. I continued by explaining how the graduate assistants and I were delivering the psychological services to the system, and why it was in the board's best interest to continue it. My armpits were wet with sweat. To save time, I began to speak more rapidly.

While I was in the middle of a sentence, one board member abruptly asked the superintendent, "When is this young man going to finish? I'm missing Bonanza."

Turning his head to face me and with a flip of his hand, the superintendent said to me, "Yes, you need to finish up soon."

"Yes, sir," came my reply.

I still had a lot of details I needed to explain about how the psychological records were being maintained, how many psychological evaluations had been conducted, how many teacher meetings had been attended, how many parent meetings had been held, how many multi-disciplinary team meetings had been chaired and much more if the board was going to understand what a bargain they were getting through the cooperative.

As I was rapidly covering these important details, the school board member who had said that he was missing his favorite TV program slowly got out of his chair, walked in front of me as he then turned to walk the length of the basketball court to the outside door.

I did not miss a beat in my presentation as this happened. Suddenly the superintendent stood up and pointed to the exit door as he exclaimed, "He's collapsed. Jim, call an ambulance. Tom, get a bucket of water."

All of the board members were up and walking around. Several of them had rushed outside the door to provide whatever assistance they could. The superintendent was standing at his desk talking on the telephone. As I stood in front of him not knowing what to do, the superintendent put the telephone to his chest as he motioned his hand to me and stated, "Continue with your presentation. We're taking care of him."

I did as directed while he talked on the phone telling someone that the ambulance was there, and some of the board members returned to their seats. Just as soon as the superintendent cradled the phone, it would ring. He would answer it. Speaking in a loud voice he would explain the situation, then cradle the phone, then answer it again as it rang. The process was repeated multiple times.

My presentation was completed shortly after the ambulance left with its patient and most of the board members had returned to mill around their chairs. At last, I had said all that I had intended to say.

The superintendent, seated at his desk by this time, thanked me for the presentation and said that the board would consider my recommendations. With that, he said that I could leave and join my family. I left. A week or so later I learned that Mr. Green had been appointed to be the halftime supervisor of special education and the system was continuing its contract with the cooperative.

As time passed, I learned more about my July 1974 presentation in the hot gymnasium.

The school board member who asked when I would finish talking as he was missing Bonanza had passed out from heat exhaustion. Several years after that incident, he was appointed by that school board to be a member of the cooperative's board of directors. I quickly learned that he was a great one for making jokes. His comment on missing his favorite TV show was a joke meant to tell me and the superintendent that I needed to stop talking. It was too hot, and he was experiencing a great deal of personal discomfort. I have been told by several sources that the school system's superintendent and Mr. Fields had a long history of conflict between them. It has been quietly reported to me that the two of them constantly ran against each other for the position of superintendent at every election cycle. After many years of this competition, the superintendent and Mr. Green reached the understanding that if Mr. Green did not run against him, the superintendent would appoint Mr. Green to a comfortable supervisory position from which he could retire. I don't know if this was just a rumor or a fact. I do know that in rural school systems, just about every relationship in the system has a long history. Rural systems have a very low staff turnover rate. A high number of school staff have lived in the surrounding community their entire lives, as have their parents, grandparents, aunts, uncles and siblings.

Two final bits of history to this story that I have learned may be of interest. The superintendent was defeated in the next election, and Mr. Green retired shortly thereafter. The outstanding graduate assistant's mother had been a former classmate of Mr. Green when they were children attending the same school. They knew each other well. Mr. Green knew the graduate assistant, Doug, as a child. For a few years, Doug had attended a school where Mr. Green taught.

Until I had learned otherwise, I did use the humor found in the comment that my detailed presentation was keeping the board member from watching his favorite TV show. However, the most important lesson I learned about being the new person initiating change in school systems was that each system has a long history of personal relationships. It would have been helpful for me to know the history of every one of my school systems before I had started working with them, but that was not possible. At best, the change agent has to be aware that historical relationships are present and be ready to recognize them as quickly as possible so that appropriate adjustments can be made.

Since the time of that presentation, I have learned to be as brief as possible when speaking to school board members, at cooperative board of directors meetings and with other groups. Yet, I have continued to be reminded that I tend to provide more details in my presentations than is necessary.

Now that decades have passed since that first year, 1973-1974, of our work at the educational cooperative, I can share some of the background information I learned about the events described above. It took many years for me to acquire these understandings. Some individuals told me that the standard operating procedure of that superintendent and school board was to decide issues about to be discussed at a board meeting before the meetings were held. Everyone understood what the decisions were going to be concerning the issues to be discussed before the meeting took place. The meeting was simply a public formality. The school system had already decided to appoint Mr. Green to be the supervisor of special education before my presentation, and Mr. Green knew that the decision had been made. I was the only one who did not understand that fact at the time.

In the early spring of that first year, another situation arose that contained an important cultural lesson for me. As I was leaving the Blount County Courthouse from a meeting with some of Blount County School officials to get my car in the adjacent parking lot, someone called out my name. Turning, I saw a senior supervisor I knew from the school system. Quickly, he walked up to me and began poking me vigorously in the chest with his finger as he shouted, "Why are you destroying Tim's special education program?"

I was stunned. I didn't know what he was talking about. "What? I don't understand. I am not trying to do that. What do you mean?"

"You know exactly what I mean. Your psychologists are not filling his retarded classes. Instead, they are identifying kids that Tim doesn't have any teachers for."

"Well, your system has done an excellent job of identifying moderately intellectually disabled students. You have nine classrooms of them. For a system of your size that is an accomplishment to be proud of. You have already identified the vast majority of that student population. This is the first time your system has been looking at children with other disabilities like learning disabilities and behavioral disorders. That's why the psych interns are finding them instead."

"Don't tell me that! Your psychologists are only writing in their reports what you tell them to write."

"That's not true!"

"It is!" he angrily stated as he walked away.

Wow, I thought, he thinks everyone in his system does exactly as he tells them to do. If they don't, he will see to it that they are removed. He does not understand the concept of professionalism within the practice of school psychology or within the teaching profession.

I was to encounter this lack of understanding within the educational setting by some supervisors and in other educators over the years as well as from the communities of the various school systems.

The importance of the communities' understanding the changes imposed on their school systems by the new special education laws was demonstrated in a meeting with the superintendent of Lenoir City Schools, located in Loudon County, during the middle of 1974-1975 school year. He had requested that both the highly regarded school psychology graduate assistant serving his system and I meet with him.

In the meeting he wanted to know if he really had to follow all of the requirements in the state and federal special education laws. Yes, he had to follow them. We explained the consequences to the system if he didn't. There would be parents who would request a due process hearing. The hearing officer would rule against the school system. If the system still refused to implement the requirements of the laws, the parents could take the case to state or federal court. The courts would rule against the system. If the system still refused to implement the laws, the state and the federal government would withhold their funding to the system. The parents would, in turn, sue the system and win.

Another example of this lack of understanding comes from an East Tennessee school system that was not a member of the cooperative but had contracted for a school psychology intern to deliver psychological services a few days a week. Midway through that school year, that system's supervisor of special education requested that the intern not be present at the more routine presentations of the psychological reports to a child's parents. On many occasions, the graduate assistant's presence needlessly increased the cost of psych services to the system, he noted. That increase was in mileage reimbursement for travel from the cooperative's office to and then from the school system. Sometimes it also required the intern to work an extra day due to scheduling problems. That was another increase in cost to the system. I spoke with the intern concerning the system's request. This was an unusual request since it was the cooperative's standard operating procedure to always have the psychological service provider present when their testing report was presented to a parent. The intern agreed that on routine evaluation results, the system could adequately explain them. We both agreed that the intern would be the one to decide which reports fit that description with specific sets of parents. The school system agreed to that condition.

A month or two after the system began presenting routine psychological reports to parents without the psychological service provider being present, that provider asked for an immediate meeting with me. She reported that the school system was giving false information to parents about the results of the psychological evaluation of their children. Right then, I called the supervisor of special education to ask if this was true. He said it was. I told him that it would have to stop. He said that he would not do that. I told him that it was illegal and we could not allow it to continue. I asked why he thought he could do it. His reply was that was the way they did things in his system. I told him that we would discontinue the service if he persisted. He said that he was not going to change his stance. That was it. We both agreed that the cooperative's delivery of psychological services to his system was terminated as of this telephone call.

Fortunately, that year the co-op had the funds to continue paying the monthly reimbursement to the intern for assistance in the central office while we looked for other opportunities for her. Very quickly, one of the member school systems gladly added her scheduled time to their contract for psych services. A year later, I learned that a nearby agency had agreed to deliver psych services to the obstructive system. The director of that agency's psychological services was a personal friend. He knew of our conflict with that system and insisted that the mistakes of the past could not be repeated. The system agreed and followed the correct procedures.

In another situation, a teacher was a member of an independent advisory board to a project funded by a grant managed by the cooperative. The director of that project needed to be terminated from that position for violating conditions of the grant. Among other things, the approval of removing her would be enhanced if the advisory board agreed that the person's position should be terminated. The assistant superintendent of the system the teacher came from was also in attendance at the board meeting and had a right to vote on the issue.

After I presented my reasons for the termination and the director had an opportunity to respond, the vote was taken. The vast majority of the advisory board voted in support of my recommendation, including the assistant superintendent. The teacher from that same school system voted against my recommendation. After the meeting the assistant superintendent angrily approached the teacher to instruct her in no uncertain terms that she was never to vote against the school system's administration again. I did not listen to their conversation but noted that it appeared to end on a more pleasant note than it had begun.

To many school administrators, the concept of professionalism in education is not a reality. Doctoral level school psychologists usually have met their state's requirements to apply for a professional license to practice psychology issued by the state's board of healing arts. This is the same board that licenses physicians to practice medicine. The license of a doctoral school psychologist is the same level of licensure as the licensure of a medical doctor. Would a school system administrator who feels free to change a school psychologist's report also feel free to change the system's medical doctor's report on a child found to have cancer? Of course not. Why do these educators think that their employees are not professionals with codes of conduct and ethics? Just because these employees are certified by their state's department of education does not remove their credentials from the ranks of professionals nor all of the accompanying ethical responsibilities. This applies to their behavior as well.

A larger number of professional administrators function as professionals than those who do not. The following is an example of what I mean. A few years after the cooperative had been delivering psychological services to the systems, it had added the service of speech therapy. The speech therapist providing services to Monroe County Schools was in the process of obtaining her "three C's," the Certification of Clinical Competence. Achieving this level would allow the therapist to be fully credentialed as a speech therapist enabling the person to be licensed by a state's board of healing arts and go into private practice.

One of the requirements for obtaining the three C's was to be under a year of supervision from a licensed speech therapist (one who has her three C's). The cooperative did not have a licensed speech therapist under its employment. Its speech therapists were certified as such by the state's department of education. This meant that the speech therapist could function in school systems. It did not mean that the speech therapist could deliver such services outside of the school system to the public. The only way that could happen is if the school system's speech therapist were also licensed.

One of the ethical requirements of a speech therapist whether the person was certified or licensed is that the therapist cannot knowingly deliver services that do not improve the patient's condition. This safeguards the public and school systems from unwarranted charges. It saves them from unethical behavior.

It so happened that after several months of speech therapy, one child receiving speech therapy had not improved. The speech therapist had informed the Three C's supervising licensed speech therapist of this fact. Several different strategies were then tried with the same results, no improvement. The speech therapist had kept me informed of this problem and the efforts made to find other strategies that might bring about improvements in the child's issues. Finally, the therapist informed me that the speech therapy sessions to the child would be terminated. The school system's administration was informed of this. A meeting was scheduled to inform the child's parents that the therapy sessions would be ending because the child no longer benefitted from them. The parents were outraged. They did not want the sessions to stop. They would not accept any explanation for why they had to stop. Finally, the parents demanded that they appeal to the system's school board.

I attended that meeting and presented the speech therapists' reason for discontinuing the service. I presented all of the testing that determined that the child was not benefiting from the service. Nothing would satisfy the parents or the grandfather of the child. Finally, near me and across the meeting table stood the grandfather shaking his finger at me as he shouted, "I'll kill you! If I'd brought my gun to this meeting, I'd be shooting you right now!" The school system administration immediately stood up and surrounded the man trying to calm him as he continued his tirade. Quietly, the system's school social worker leaned over to me and said, "You need to leave. We'll handle this." I left. No one spoke of the incident to me after that night. The speech therapy sessions for that child did not resume. The school system respected and protected its professionals.

The cooperative's policy has always been to maintain professional standards and professional behaviors regardless of any threats to the existence of the cooperative or its programs. Some of the challenges to this position will be discussed later.

In the 1979 qualitative study of the cooperative conducted by the University of Illinois, a section is titled, Better Years, (pages 28 to 30), reflects the understanding gained from interviews and research of the beginning impact of the cooperative's psychological and special education services delivery model starting in 1973.

PG. 28:

BETTER YEARS

With 1973 dawned the beginning of a new era for the Co-op. That year, Tennessee Public Law 839 came into effect along with additional state funding to hasten compliance. The law established as state policy to require school districts to provide special education services sufficient to meet the needs and maximize the capabilities of handicapped children.

This new mandate loomed large and threatening for most school districts. First, the state did not interpret the law, nor did it prescribe the logistics of how compliance might occur. Secondly, the educational implications of the law ran contrary to the existing fabric of schooling being practiced by many districts. As one observer put it, "The law was antithetical to the educational system in the state—a bureaucracy in which educators run the show.

The seven LTVEC districts were sufficiently alarmed about the prospects of the new legislation for educating the handicapped to agree to the cooperative pooling of resources in order that the Co-op might develop a full-scale psychological service program, complete with an added staff person to see to its success. Subsequently, this person, Dr. Jerry Morton, was hired. He immediately embarked upon a mission to successfully utilize the Handicapped Education Law, with its encumbrances and benefits, as a vehicle for pulling the Cooperative together, strengthening programs, enlarging staff, balancing the budget, and shaping a new dream for the Co-op, a dream which was to include words like "individualized instruction," "advocacy for children," "development of human resources," and "educational revolution."

PG. 29

The new Psychological Services program included two major thrusts. First, a cadre of University of Tennessee graduate students in psychology were hired on a part-time basis to go about doing outreach work in testing and placement for the school districts. This group not only achieved delivery of services to schools but they also quadrupled the Co-op staff and generally infiltrated the ranks with youthful idealism and priorities which placed concern for handicapped children above concerns for agency, districts, power, politics, and economics.

In the second thrust of the new psychological services program, Jerry Morton began to work personally with the Co-op districts in arriving at viable interpretation of Law 839, in providing badly needed legal assistance and consultation to the districts themselves.

The perceived utility to districts of the Psychological Services Program over the past six years is readily documented across the several districts:

Monroe County:

"About six years ago we began our program of individualized instruction. We're about halfway there; the Handicapped Program has helped a lot. Our whole intent is not for the accelerated but for the lagging child. We have been guilty of teaching to the mass. Public Law 839 really puts focus on the lagging child."

Blount County:

"It [assistance from the Co-op] was very necessary at the beginning. We wouldn't have been able to do the things we have done without Psych Services. It [839] hit us, and we didn't have the people.

It was necessary that we have supervision... interpretation of the law was a big thing with us on that."

Loudon County:

"Loudon County hadn't done too much for compliance. We weren't geared up to do it. Then through the Co-op, we could better meet requirements."

Lenoir City:

"We not only meet the state requirements, but I feel comfortable with it. The fact that Jerry is

PG. 30

in the background... in hearings...his expertise in general...Everybody has a high point with the Co-op. That's mine...These people will be at my side if I go to court."

With the implementation of the Psychological Services Program also came a significant shift in financial structure of the Cooperative. The member districts who had previously subscribed on a service-by-service basis were now obligated to an across-the-board commitment to share Co-op administrative and clerical costs.

As Psychological Services moved to a predominant role in the program and funding of the Co-op, a shift in leadership occurred, as well. Jerry Morton increasingly became the central leadership figure of the Co-op, with Bill Oakes moving to a figurehead role until his death in 1976, when Jerry Morton was officially appointed as LTVEC Director. The dominance of Psychological Services over other aspects of the Co-op was reflected in the Board's decision to maintain Jerry Morton as full-time Director of Psychological Services, and to simply tack on an additional $3,000 to that salary to cover additional responsibilities as Co-op director.

The districts began to experience benefits from membership in LTVEC, as the Co-op increasingly enjoyed a surge of renewed credibility and fiscal feasibility. In an interesting new twist, an outside intrusion (Public Law 839), in which promises by the outside agent were kept, a reciprocal relationship was shaped which benefitted the districts and thereby revitalized the Co-op. Or as Mac McDowell of Monroe County puts it, "*Public Law 839 became the life-saver for financing the Co-op, but the Co-op was the life saver for the school systems.*"

TEN
INCREASING NEEDS FOR A VARIETY OF SERVICES

During the first school year, 1973-74, of the cooperative's psychological and special education service delivery model, it became obvious that the member school systems needed more school psychology interns as well as an increase in time from the special education consultant in assisting the regular education staff as they implemented teaching strategies to accommodate the needs of the wide variety of disabilities children within their classrooms possessed. New arrivals also increased the needs. Some of the children needed simple adjustments. Those with vision problems might simply need to sit in the front of the classroom so that they could see the writing on the blackboard. That strategy would work as well for the moderately hearing-impaired. Other disabilities might require more complex changes within the classroom. If a child needed to be in a wheelchair all day, accommodations must be made such as widening the entrance to the classroom and ensuring that all that student's classes were on the first floor. A certified speech therapist might need to provide targeted speech therapy for students with speech difficulties. That would mean the student would have to leave the classroom for an hour a couple of times a week. How was the student going to keep up with the rest of the class when an hour of instruction was missed? We certainly did not want to give the student failing grades simply because the child missed two hours of classroom instruction a week.

Remember, prior to the 1973-74 school year, a system could simply say to a child's parents, "Your child can't come to school because we don't educate children in wheelchairs." If a child did not fit the definition of "normal" a particular school system held, then that child could not receive a free public-school education. On behalf of school systems across the country, the vast majority of school systems did make accommodations for children with a variety of "not normal" issues. Without articulating it, but behaviorally manifesting it, the definition most school systems had for the "normal" child was a child who was reading the classroom material and progressing through it at the rate that the teacher taught it day after day until the end of the school year. Then the child would be promoted to the next grade level, ready to learn what was to be taught on day one and to learn at the daily rate in which new material was taught and on and on until graduation. If the child was not ready to learn what was to be taught on day one or could not learn at the rate the new material was presented, then someone needed to fix the child so that he would learn at the "normal" rate when he entered the classroom. If the student missed a lot of school due to illness or being "fixed to be normal" the child should return ready to learn the material being taught on that day and maintain learning at the rate new material was presented. Of course, this meant that the child had managed to learn the material that was taught while school days were missed. For the gifted child who already knew the material being taught, she had to sit silently and be bored. If she complained or "acted up," she would be punished.

This belief system incorporated the concept that the responsibility of the school system was to present to the classroom teacher children who were ready to learn what she was going to teach and at the rate she taught. The children had to also know how to sit quietly in their seats and follow instructions. This set of belief systems has been so ingrained into the educational culture it never needed to be clearly articulated. It presented an invisible barrier to students with disabilities. One of the easiest points of contention between this belief system and serving children with special needs could be found in a child with a speech disability being pulled out of the classroom a couple of hours a week. How was the child going to be able to learn the material taught while she was in speech therapy?

The special education law mandated that the school system was going to have to fully accommodate the special needs child in order for that child to receive an appropriate education equal to that of "normal" children. In order to accomplish the task, some changes would be required of the teacher and that teacher would need support from the school system in order to be successful. Fortunately, these types of problems can be and are overcome through the naturally innovative characteristics possessed by successful educators as well as those professionals trained to assist them such as school psychologists, behavior analysts, guidance counselors, reading teachers, vision mobility therapists, etc.

I cannot emphasize enough the collective quality and effectiveness that existed in the teaching staff employed by the school systems in the cooperative. The creative teaching strategies developed by individual teachers to work around the learning blocks of the children with disabilities are reflected in the book mentioned earlier, *What's Cooking in the Classroom*.

During the first year of the implementation of the special education law, extra funds were provided to identify those children with disabilities that negatively affected their regular education. The second year, and in following years, extra funds were provided school systems to provide special education services to the identified children. Granted, the funds for the first and second years of special education law implementation were never enough to cover the extra costs fully, but they were more than the systems had ever received before. The local school systems had to make up the difference between the funds provided by the state and the federal government. This created serious tensions for rural communities with a limited tax base. The consequences to a school system for not adequately educating a disabled child was having to defend their actions in a due process hearing. A due process hearing could be requested by any parent of a disabled or suspected disabled child. If the due process hearing officer ruled in favor of the parents' position, the school system had the option of appealing the decision in court. This was a costly process to the system both in staff time and money. Sometimes the biggest cost to the system could be the loss of community support for the school system and its leaders.

A variety of specialized professionals were needed by the school systems to serve many of their children with disabilities. Each system's needs often did not require a full-time specialist in a certain field, and they could not afford to employ one on a full-time basis when there was only a part-time need. This remains particularly true for small rural school systems. Once again, the educational cooperative was the perfect tool to assist the systems to meet the needs of their children in that one specialist could serve children in more than one school system. One of the first identified specialized services needed was speech therapy. Shortly thereafter, the need for physical and occupational therapists was recognized. As the years passed, the need for more specialized service providers would become apparent. This was particularly true for the child with behavioral difficulties. The problem for the educational establishment in dealing with mental health issues was and is so complex that I'll need to address it as a separate issue later.

In the 1970's and beyond, there were significant issues to overcome in employing specialized professionals to serve children within a school environment. To start with, not enough qualified speech therapists or other types of therapists were available to meet the demand for their services. The training centers for these specialists were located at the state's major universities, which were located in the major population centers. The large cities had hospitals and clinics that employed the licensed specialists. Their training programs were not geared to prepare them to understand and work within a school environment. In addition, specialists were reluctant to drive long distances to work in environments with which they were unfamiliar to be the only specialist in their field providing services in a setting that might be hostile to the services they provide. The educational cooperative was a natural vehicle for overcoming these obstacles.

The cooperative was a collection of professionals with specialized skills. It provided an emotional support base for the therapists. It could and did employ several credentialed therapists such as speech therapists who were each the sole provider of speech therapy to a few children in a single school system for half a day and in another system for two days and in another system for a period of time as the result of being a full-time employee of the co-op. Once a difficult case was before the speech therapist, she could consult with the co-op's other speech therapists to work collectively in discovering the best way of assisting a child. In turn, the speech therapist might overhear an educator whisper to another something like, "Schools aren't hospitals. It's just a waste of money having a speech therapist work with that child. I know her parents. That kid will never learn."

When something like that is heard, it's easy to get depressed. You may just not want to return. Through the cooperative you can discuss the situation with a colleague. That person understands and can help you gain perspective. Besides, you had helped her with resolving a depressing situation earlier. The cooperative structure provides a support system for the professionals working in environments that don't fully understand or appreciate the therapists' specialized skills. That support system exists because the cooperative knows how to provide it and does.

The power of speech therapy provided directly in the schools is demonstrated by the fact that today it is just about impossible to encounter a child who stutters by fourth grade. Anyone who attended grade school from the 1940's through the mid 1970's can remember someone in school who stuttered. We all owe our thanks to speech therapists and the special education laws of today. The same can be said for all the other specialized therapists working within the educational environment.

In addition to the cooperative beginning to expand its special education services to the member schools through the employment of speech, physical and occupational therapists, it began writing and winning national and state education grants. The grants were those in which the vast majority of applications were rejected. The awarding of the grants was based on merit. All identifying information of the applicant was removed from the grant. Thus the grant readers could not bring various biases into their evaluation of each proposal. This ensured that the grants were awarded on the basis of merit rather than on political or other unrelated issues.

The first federal grant awarded to the coop came in 1975. "Project Talent Development" was funded by the U. S. Office of Education as a Title IV-C grant. The grant was for three years. It provided the cooperative with new staff to work in the area of providing enrichment programs to gifted students within the co-op's seven-member school systems. In turn, what was learned from the implementation of the grant's strategies was reported to the grantor for distribution to other school systems across the state and country. The seven or so percent of the funds allocated for administrative purposes was a true asset to the cooperative. Naturally, there were annual progress reports and end-of-project reports to file. These reports include detailed, accurate expenditure reports. The cooperative conducted a yearly audit of the federal funds to prove that the money had been properly spent only in the categories designated by the grant. It was a separate audit of the cooperative's activities. As time passed, it became routine for the cooperative to prepare seven or more separate audits to meet the requirements of various funding sources.

In 1977, the cooperative received a two-year grant from the Washington office of environmental education. Again, the administrative allowance was beneficial to the cost of operating the organization. This was the grant that contracted with Drs. Stake and Brown, University of Illinois at Urbana-Champaign, to conduct a qualitative evaluation of the cooperative's activities that were funded by the grant. As referenced earlier, Claire Brown spent eighteen days in the cooperative's area compiling the information for their report. The grant brought administrators, political leaders, teachers and students together to explore environmental issues of the region. In turn, the group made recommendations for better educating others on the issues and working together to find ways to resolve them effectively.

Another three-year grant awarded in 1979 was a Preschool Incentive Grant titled, "Preschool Identification, Cooperative Services and Parent Awareness Grant for Handicapped Children." This grant launched the cooperative's involvement in early childhood intervention programs. In the beginning, the program began serving birth-to-three-year-olds with disabilities and their families. The school systems were required by law to create early intervention programs for children with disabilities at the age of three through five. At six years old, the child would enter the school system's regular educational programming provided to all children. The data collected by the cooperative clearly demonstrated that addressing a child's disabilities in a targeted birth-to-three program promoted such improvements in the educational functioning that the member school systems allowed the cooperative to pay the costs of the program's staff for such expenses as Social Security, Medicare (FICA) and state retirement. The supervisors of special education within the member systems had documented the cost-savings of the cooperative's Birth-to-Three program. The FICA costs were paid by the co-op for decades until the program began generating the funds to cover this expense.

Over the years, the cooperative continued to receive grants from a wide range of funding sources. Data was always collected on the results of those grants and reported to various authorities. The positive gains did not always generate continuation funds, but the information gained in providing services to children with special needs continued to make an impact over many years. Sometimes the cooperative did not receive the credit for those contributions. The cooperative staff, as a collective whole, considered the fact that the ideas were adopted and implemented to be more important than to receive the credit for them. Admittedly, it would have been nice to have received the credit and the opportunity to implement the new knowledge base strategies. Again, the cooperative's perceived mission has always been in making the world a better place for our children. That goal takes precedence over all others.

Through the grants and other activities, the cooperative staff has played significant roles in the creation of parent organizations on behalf of children. These include the creation of advocacy associations for gifted children, for early intervention programs, for autism and for young adults with disabilities who have aged out of the school systems' special education programs when the special needs students turn twenty-one.

The grants have also promoted the writing and publishing of scholarly papers. One such paper, "Insights: Assisting Intellectually Gifted Students with Emotional Difficulties," was published in *Roper Review* (Vol. 1, No.2, pp. 16-18) and was included in Barbe and Renzulli's *Psychology and Education of the Gifted* (1981, Irvington Publishers, Inc., New York). At least eight academic books contain descriptions of educational programs that were developed by cooperative staff. The state and national presentations at various conferences by cooperative staff are simply too numerous to count.

The cooperative's Birth-to-Three program received the National Rural and Small Schools Consortium's 1986 Exemplary Preschool Award. Over the years other LTVEC programs have received regional and national awards as well as other types of recognition. Collectively, the awards and recognition are a verification of the fact that the educational cooperative is dedicated to high quality professional services to children and to those who serve our children.

Yet, in all of the early years of the cooperative, it was never a surety that the cooperative would have the funds necessary to continue into the next year. Each year voices were raised calling for one or more school systems to withdraw from the cooperative or to refuse to receive significant services from it. These uncertainties persisted for decades. The reasons for the criticisms need to be explored. The criticisms reflect significant cultural issues that appear in many organizations which depend upon cooperative behavior in order to survive.

Despite the annual uncertainty of the cooperative's survival, the cooperative had significant success in recruiting and retaining professional staff. With the school systems entering the pool of employers seeking the services of specialized therapists, there was a regional shortage of these professionals. Two key elements played a positive role in the cooperative's success. One was the strong desire of the therapists to work with children in educational settings. The other factor was the emphasis of the cooperative's focus on providing emotional and professional support for its service providers. The desire of the cooperative's staff to remain working with it was so strong that the various therapists often reported being offered more money to leave the cooperative and work with another agency. The therapists reported that they had refused those offers.

ELEVEN
ADJUSTING TO THE ATTACKS

The desire to "own" the service provider was much stronger than I had realized. The anger and fear displayed by many teachers and administrators during that first year of the law, 1973-1974 was understandable, and the service providers were somewhat prepared for it. The attack on the quality of the psychological services staff as individuals was not fully understood. The cooperative was seen as the agent which brought the "bad" school psychologists into their system. As noted earlier, some thought that the doctoral graduate assistants were changing the actual test results to fit what the cooperative's director of psychological services told them to put in their reports rather than reporting the truth. He was doing that out of "mean spirited behavior."

In one case, an elementary school principal reported, with great anger, that the psych intern rarely showed up at her school on the scheduled days. When I spoke to the graduate student, the accusation was vigorously denied. In confusion, the graduate assistant reported that the principal always greeted her when she first arrived at the school. The intern had never missed an assigned day. Upon further investigation the truth of the situation was discovered.

When the school psych service provider would arrive at the school early each morning, the sun was shining brightly through a window behind the school secretary's desk into the doorway of the principal's office. The principal often stood in that doorway greeting parents and other adults who would be standing at the secretary's desk. The principal always had pleasant exchanges with the visitors. She could only see the outline of the visitor's body as it was silhouetted in the brilliance of the sunlight spilling through the window behind the individual and glaring into her eyes. Complicating the recognition pattern presented by the silhouette of the graduate assistant was the fact that the graduate assistant often wore different wigs. It was learned from the secretary that the principal had an overall vision problem that she had been trying to resolve but had been unsuccessful in doing so.

The solution to the misidentification problem was resolved in such a manner that it did not embarrass the principal. Each morning when the graduate assistant arrived at the school, she asked the secretary if she could leave a brightly colored tote bag on a table in the office. When that distinctive tote bag was on the table, the principal knew the psychological service provider was there. However, the principal still found issues to point out concerning flaws in the service provider to prove that her school system should terminate all contact with the cooperative. Interestingly, when the service provider was about to receive her doctorate in psychology, become a licensed psychologist and move to another state to function in a private practice capacity, the principal pleaded with the cooperative to retain her because she was such an outstanding school psychologist.

This theme was a consistent one. In another situation, a highly regarded guidance counselor asked a supervisor in her system, Blount County Schools, to inquire if I, as a licensed psychologist, would provide her with a year's supervision while she functioned as a school psychology intern in her school system. She had completed all of the required courses and other requirements needed to be certified as a school psychologist by the state except the supervised internship requirement. I agreed. This person was simply outstanding. She was well-known by many in the school system and highly valued for her ability to work with teachers and children. I quickly learned that the high regard others had for her was valid. After she had completed the internship requirements, she received her certification. At that time the school system provided the cooperative with the funds to employ this individual as a full-time school psychologist.

We continued to meet on a regularly scheduled basis and at staff meetings. We would discuss strategies for assisting specific children with unusual difficulties. Again, this person was an outstanding school psychologist. In the late spring, she approached me to say that she was going to resign her position through the cooperative for the coming year. She would be employed directly by her school system as their school psychologist serving the same schools she had while with the cooperative. I supported her in her decision but was confused as to why she did not want to continue working through the cooperative. She teared up as she explained that the cooperative was such a professionally supportive organization that she would have preferred to have stayed, but she simply could not emotionally withstand the constant criticism she received from the schools as one of those "no good" cooperative people. The next year I would indirectly receive reports from that system about how good a school psychologist she was. I was confident that those reports were correct.

The issue was with the cooperative. It was not with the individual service provider. This lesson was repeated time and time again. When a cooperative's school system built up enough of a need for a full-time school psychologist and the cooperative's graduate assistant was graduating, the system would terminate the contract for psychological services through the coop for the reason that the cooperative was falling short in providing adequate service providers. Time and time again, the system would then offer their school psychologist position to the same service provider that the cooperative had been employing on their behalf. The issue was control. The issue was pride. The issue was demonstrating that the system did not need "outsiders" to serve their children as well as many other issues neither the system nor the cooperative could articulate or understand. The system wanted to have their "own" service providers.

The cooperative's financial survival was based upon delivering professional services through the school systems to their children. The question became, could the cooperative serve as a training ground in the development of service providers who, after proving themselves, became employed directly by the systems in which they had been trained? The needs of the systems were such that in the later years of the 1970's they began realizing that they needed other specialized services. Circumstances did not permit them to employ these professionals (speech therapists, physical therapists, occupational therapists, vision specialists, mobility specialists, etc.) directly. This was where the cooperative could help them. At least for a while, as the number of psychological service providers employed by the cooperative decreased, the number of specialists in other areas increased. This transition did not begin in earnest until the early 1980s.

As reported earlier, the member systems were concerned that one system would get a greater quantity of a service than the others were receiving at the expense of those systems. They did not want the funds they were providing to the cooperative to serve their children to be diverted to provide services to children in another school system. While the cooperative provided detailed monthly records of the services delivered to each system and to other member systems, there were challenges from time to time. They were quickly explained. The cooperative never misused funds and went to great effort to collect records that proved this fact. Unfortunately, I was to learn that this type of concern was a real one in other cooperatives. I'll address this in more detail later.

Many times, when a member system had a new superintendent, supervisor of special education, school principal, school board member or the like, the issue of funds being sent to the cooperative was raised. Sometimes, the new authority figure did not want to receive the correct information concerning LTVEC's activities as it conflicted with their beliefs. It was important that all of the cooperative staff respond to these challenges with respect and patience.

A common occurrence arose when a new school board member was first confronted with a discrepancy between the need to improve services in their system and the shortage of funds to provide those services. The new board member would look at their system's overall budget and see the line item for the cooperative. The immediate recommendation was to simply stop paying LTVEC and use those funds to address the pressing needs within the system. It took patience and respect for the school board member's perspective to explain that the services provided by the cooperative would cost the system more if it tried to deliver them on its own if that were even possible. The system needed the cooperative. More often than not, the school board member would end up being a strong supporter of the cooperative.

Another concern of the member systems was the administrative costs of operating the coop. In the beginning, the systems were paying a membership fee based upon the percentage of their student population as compared to the combined student population. That fee paid the salaries for the executive director and the bookkeeper/office manager/secretary. It also covered their office costs (phone, typewriters, mileage and travel expenses, etc.) and I assume paying down the bank loans. When the psychological and special education services component began in 1973, the administrative costs for that component were included in the charges for the overall service as a self-contained division. Those costs included the salaries of the program director and the secretary. It also included the support costs of maintaining the office (telephone system for staff, communication expenses, postage, travel reimbursement for staff, typewriter, paper, etc.). I don't remember the exact percentage of the administrative costs for psychological services and special education, but it was around twelve percent. This was a major concern of the systems. They wanted to pay only for direct services rather than any administrative costs. The board required periodic reviews throughout the year of the administrative costs and examined them carefully. Every budget projection was required to have a separate item listing the administration costs they would have to pay.

Until around 1994, the member school systems donated space for the cooperative to house its central offices. From 1973 to around 1977, Alcoa City Schools donated space for the cooperative. Because of the school system's growth, it needed the rooms that had been provided to LTVEC. Blount County Schools graciously agreed to donate office space in their Maryville location of the old Everett High School's gym building. A new high school had been built to serve the students that had attended the former Everett High School. Another building also on the campus contained the system's special education center which served children with significant disabling conditions into their adolescent years.

When that school system withdrew their membership from the cooperative in 1982, the Loudon County/Lenoir City Vocational Education Center donated office space for the cooperative's use. Around 1992 the vocational center needed that space because of their increase in student population. At that time, none of the member systems were able to provide office space for the cooperative. Thus, the cooperative had to rent office space. Along with the cost of the rent came the cost for electricity, heating/cooling, cleaning and advertising the location. Those expenses significantly increased the administrative cost for the member school systems. Of course, the administrative costs per system increased when the largest school system withdrew its membership.

The administrative cost and subsequent percentage of the total budget would fluctuate with the increase in services the systems obtained through the cooperative. While the office space was being donated, the administrative costs were considerably lower. In 1976 when I became the director, we combined the administrative costs of the central office and the direct services into one unit. The administrative salary for the full-time director became reduced to a three-thousand- dollar supplement to my salary as the director of the direct services component. That left the salary of the bookkeeper/office manager and related support costs as added administrative costs to the direct services costs. The total increase was minimal, as the bank loan had been repaid by that time.

As the member systems increased the professional services they were purchasing from the cooperative, a financial surplus began to develop at the end of the fiscal year. LTVEC adopted the policy that for every administrative dollar collected from a member school system, the membership fee would be equally reduced. In a few years no need existed to assign a membership fee to any of the school systems. The LTVEC board dropped the membership fee altogether by the early 1980s. Once the cooperative had to pay office rent and support costs, the administrative charges would fluctuate between seventeen and twenty-five percent of the total charge for a service. The fluctuation would depend on the number of services being purchased through the co-op. The larger the amount of funds provided to LTVEC for services, the lower the administrative fee became. As a result of the talented support staff working with LTVEC and their insightful problem-solving skills, the number of salaried staff supporting the cooperative's programs remained remarkably constant over the years.

The member systems insisted that the administrative cost be listed as a line item in any budget projected or contract established with any organization. The charge of twenty some percent for administrative costs was considered to be outrageous by some school systems. Supervisors of special education services could understand being charged the cost of a professional service provider's salary. That was the cornerstone for them in determining how many staff they could employ. Their superintendent would allocate a set amount of funds they could spend on salaries. When they prepared their department's budget, it was the combined salaries of their staff. They did not have to include the FICA costs, the cost of the bond issue being paid for building the school buildings, their salary as the supervisor, the heating and cooling costs for the office space the staff was in, etc. The school system's central office paid those costs directly. When the cooperative prepared a budget for the supervisor of a special education division of a school system for a speech therapist, that figure would include the therapist's salary for the number of days she would be working in the system and then added a charge of twenty some percent as an administrative charge. Some supervisors considered that outrageous.

At a regional education conference I attended near Knoxville, a discussion session I attended was exploring the difficulties in finding a licensed specialist to work just a day or two in school systems. I spoke up to say that an organization like the cooperative could help solve that problem. A high-level supervisor from a large school system stood up and angrily informed the group that yes, the cooperative could do that, but then it would add a twenty-five administrative cost to however much it would cost to hire the professional. I tried to respond. Before I could do so in detail, the time for the session to end had arrived. I happened to have read earlier in a local newspaper that a study had been conducted on the administrative costs of the system the critic came from. That system's administrative costs were over sixty percent. Out of every education dollar spent, more than sixty cents was spent on administrative costs. There were the salaries of the superintendent, the assistant superintendent, the supervisors out of the central office, the principal of the school building, the vice-principal and then there were the salaries of all of the secretaries at all of the levels of administration, the maintenance staff, the lunchroom staff.

All of those salaried school support staff for the classroom teacher had to have the system pay the administration's part into the educator retirement system as well as paying the employer's share of the payroll and Medicare taxes. Then expenses for supporting the school building included such things as building maintenance, phone service, the electric bill, the heating/cooling bill and the debt encumbered from loans to pay for the construction of the school building. I haven't gotten into the cost of insurance or school bus expenses. It is easy to understand why so many educational administrators look older than their actual age. By comparison, the cooperative's administrative costs were a true bargain compared to those of a fully functioning school system. Yet, to those who never have to think about those things, the cooperative's charge of seventeen to twenty-five percent for those expenses is outrageous. The cooperative staff has to patiently explain these issues to those decision makers who do not understand.

Once the cooperative's budget was set for the next school year and the administrative fee was established, the question of the cooperative's survival was no longer raised. Most years, during my forty-one years with the cooperative, the answer was not firmly known until May or June. The fact that the cooperative's staff continued to stay committed to it that close to the start of the next school year, July 1, speaks highly of their feeling connected to the mission of the co-op, their commitment to the delivery model for services the cooperative had developed, to the co-op staff they worked with and the effectiveness of the co-op's focus on supporting the staff's mental health. The professional staff was often offered more money to work with other organizations but stayed because of their satisfaction with the co-op. As the school year progressed, several school systems began asking the cooperative to find certified or licensed professionals to fill positions that they were unable to fill on their own.

These highly skilled professionals were often found and would work in the schools because of the reputation the cooperative had for supporting those who worked through it. These added positions provided unexpected surpluses in the cooperative's budget. Once a large enough surplus in the budget allowed the co-op to continue paying the staff for a few months in the event that a system or granting source had to delay their obligated payments to the co-op, the question was what to do with the extra funds. The board decided to refund the school systems the surplus based upon the percentage of services each system was receiving from the cooperative. This was a way of rewarding a school system for purchasing large amounts of services from the organization. In turn, it gave the superintendents an added reason to present to their school boards as to why membership in LTVEC was a good decision. For a period of about ten years, approximately ten thousand dollars a year was returned to the member systems.

The refunding process stopped as the number of services requested by the systems decreased. The decrease took place as a result of changes in state and federal laws that allowed school systems to be reimbursed through Medicaid funds to school systems that employed qualified therapists to provide one-to-one services to children with special needs who were eligible of having those needs met through Medicaid funding. Up to that point, only private practice providers could receive those payments. With this change in the law, a child needing physical therapy three hours a week could go to a physical therapist's office for the three hours or receive the physical therapy in the school with the school's licensed physical therapist being paid by the school system and the system being reimbursed the cost by Medicaid. Medicaid paid for just the one-on-one delivery of service. It did not pay for consultations with the child's teacher on ways she could assist the child's recovery within the classroom, or for money into a retirement system for the therapist, or for any equipment the therapist might need to assist her client. This was the medical model for the delivery of services.

The education model for the delivery of services revolves around the school day. The therapist is in the school building for half a day or a full day depending on the number of children attending who need her services. She delivers the prescribed hours of one-on-one therapy, then spends time in the classroom observing how the child in question functions in order to engage the teacher in things that can be done within the classroom to support the goals of the direct face-to-face therapy. In turn, the therapist meets with the other therapists serving the child to develop more integrated strategies that will be of greater assistance to the child's progress than would otherwise be the case. Of course, there may also be an opportunity to speak with the parents as well.

The medical model only pays for one-on-one direct service to the client from the professional. The education service model is a fully integrated model as opposed to the medical one-on-one model. Overall, the medical model is cheaper than the educational model. However, over time the more integrated educational model produces faster recoveries in the special needs child than the medical one does. To the taxpayer, the educational model is the most economical one. To the school system just trying to make it from one year to the next, the medical model is cheaper. Some of the cooperative school systems that took advantage of the immediate savings to their budget the medical model provided did return to the educational model in their delivery of services to their children with disabilities.

That integrated model has proven to be the most cost effective as it provides the highest quality of service for the child. An old joke I tell to make this point is, "Let's go sky diving. It doesn't cost much. I had the parachutes packed by the low bidder." Some years after the medical model payments were made available to the school systems, it was recognized that LTVEC could receive Medicaid payments as an educational organization due to its being an extension of its member school systems. The school systems were reimbursed the Medicaid money and paid for the therapists' additional integrative work.

The cooperative's best example of the effectiveness of the integrated service delivery model is the one developed by the co-op's Birth-to-Three program for children with serious disabilities. That program started with the awarding of the three-year Preschool Incentive Grant titled, "Preschool Identification, Cooperative Services and Parent Awareness Grant for Handicapped Children" in

1979 followed by the 1981 Office of Education HCEEP Grant, "Rural Preschool Services Model Project." That grant was for three years as well. Blount County Schools provided the space for these two projects in the same building that the central offices were in.

A simple example demonstrating the concept of the integrated service delivery model follows. A two- year-old child has speech difficulties along with poor fine motor and gross motor hand and arm movements. The child's speech therapist, occupational therapist, and physical therapist as well as the child's preschool teacher meet and share the strategies each of them is using so that they can all shape their individual therapies into a supportive whole. The speech therapist is currently working on assisting the child to make "R" sounds. The occupational therapist is working to assist the child to improve her finger control by having her try to grasp objects and the physical therapist is assisting the child so that she can better use her shoulder muscles in reaching for things. The speech therapist holds a *red* ball within the reach of the child as she focuses on assisting the child to make the "R" sound while encouraging the child to reach the red ball and touch it. The physical therapist holds up a doll in a red dress to encourage the child to reach for it while noting the pretty red dress. The occupational therapist teams up with the classroom teacher encouraging the child to hold red Jello in her hand during the lunch break.

Every aspect of the child's activities is integrated to enhance the goals of the various therapists working with the child. This is a far more efficient delivery model than having the child driven from one therapist's office to another one to receive various services in isolation from each other. The child makes significant progress in far less time in the integrated services delivery model. The child's improvements are far less expensive to achieve in the integrated services delivery model.

Sometimes the cooperative staff would become confused and support mistaken ideas within the system where they were working. For example, around the late 1970's or early 1980's, two recently employed school psychology interns working in Blount County Schools approached me in an angry manner saying something like, "LTVEC is supposed to be a cooperative! Not enough school psychologists and interns are working in the Blount County Schools to meet the needs of the schools for our services. If this is a cooperative, then it should take some of the interns from the other systems and have them work here. This is where the greatest need is!"

I agreed that Blount County Schools needed more people delivering psych services. The demand was far greater than the staff could meet. I had asked the system to increase their funding to enable the co-op to provide more graduate assistants or full-time school psychologists. The request was denied. Then I explained that the other systems did not want the money they had given to the co-op to provide specific services to their children to be diverted from their children to serve Blount County School System's children. "Then this isn't a cooperative," was their reply. Technically, they were correct. The cooperative was more like a federation. In that sense, the states within the United States sometimes function more like a federation than a cooperative. Some actions that the states engaged in were independent of the others. Actions also were undertaken in a cooperative manner to the benefit of all concerned. This was also true for LTVEC.

Since the focus of my attention was on finding solutions to the problems the professional service providers were encountering and in finding ways to maintain the cooperative's financial health, the risk of a failure to recognize the successes the organization was having existed. When I started with the cooperative, Bill Oakes had told me that there were about 75 other educational cooperatives throughout the state. I learned that there were four other educational cooperatives in the East Tennessee area. Bill told me there were many of them in the western end of the state. He reported that he had been asked to join some kind of association of cooperative directors, but he didn't have the time for it nor did he see how such a group could be of assistance to LTVEC. When I became LTVEC's director, I was never contacted by such a group. There was no meaningful contact with the other cooperatives in East Tennessee. What little I knew about them indicated that they were all struggling to survive.

TWELVE
HOW IT WAS IN 1979

The purpose of the qualitative research study conducted by the University of Illinois in 1979 was to study the implementation of the environmental grant the cooperative had received from the federal government in 1978. The study evolved into being an evaluation of the cooperative as a whole. The final sections of the research project provided an analysis of the cooperative that gave a fuller perspective of the cooperative than I had had at the time. The first two paragraphs of the section titled "Better Years" of the Stake/Brown report have been covered in Chapter 4 of this book. They are repeated here as part of the entirety of this section. That perspective began on page 28 under the heading, "BETTER YEARS," and concluded on page 43. Those attached pages follow.

PG. 28

BETTER YEARS

With 1973 dawned the beginning of a new era for the Co-op. That year, Tennessee Public Law 839 came into effect along with additional state funding to hasten compliance. The law established as state policy to require school districts to provide special education services sufficient to meet the needs and maximize the capabilities of handicapped children.

This new mandate loomed large and threatening for most school districts. First, the state did not interpret the law, nor did it prescribe the logistics of how compliance might occur. Secondly, the educational implications of the law ran contrary to the existing fabric of schooling being practiced by many districts. As one observer put it, "The law was antithetical to the educational system in the state—a bureaucracy in which educators run the show.

The seven LTVEC districts were sufficiently alarmed about the prospects of the new legislation for educating the handicapped to agree to the cooperative pooling of resources in order that the Co-op might develop a full-scale psychological service program, complete with an added staff person to see to its success. Subsequently, this person, Dr. Jerry Morton, was hired. He immediately embarked upon a mission to successfully utilize the Handicapped Education Law, with its encumbrances and benefits, as a vehicle for pulling the Cooperative together, strengthening programs, enlarging staff, balancing the budget, and shaping a new dream for the Co-op, a dream which was to include words like "individualized instruction," "advocacy for children," "development of human resources," and "educational revolution."

PG. 29

The new Psychological Services program included two major thrusts. First, a cadre of University of Tennessee graduate students in psychology were hired on a part-time basis to go about doing outreach work in testing and placement for the school districts. This group not only achieved delivery of services to schools but they also quadrupled the Co-op staff and generally infiltrated the ranks with youthful idealism and priorities which placed concern for handicapped children above concerns for agency, districts, power, politics, and economics.

In the second thrust of the new psychological services program, Jerry Morton began to work personally with the Co-op districts in arriving at viable interpretation of Law 839, in providing badly needed legal assistance and consultation to the districts themselves.

The perceived utility to districts of the Psychological Services Program over the past six years is readily documented across the several districts:

Monroe County:

"About six years ago we began our program of individualized instruction. We're about halfway there; the Handicapped Program has helped a lot. Our whole intent is not for the accelerated but for the lagging child. We have been guilty of teaching to the mass. Public Law 839 really puts focus on the lagging child."

Blount County:

"It [assistance from the Co-op] was very necessary at the beginning. We wouldn't have been able to do the things we have done without Psych Services. It [839] hit us, and we didn't have the people. It was necessary that we have supervision...interpretation of the law was a big thing with us on that."

Loudon County:

"Loudon County hadn't done too much for compliance. We weren't geared up to do it. Then through the Co-op, we could better meet requirements."

Lenoir City:

"We not only meet the state requirements, but I feel comfortable with it. The fact that Jerry is

PG. 30

in the background... in hearings...his expertise in general...Everybody has a high point with the Co-op. That's mine...These people will be at my side if I go to court."

With the implementation of the Psychological Services Program also came a significant shift in financial structure of the Cooperative. The member districts who had previously subscribed on a service-by-service basis were now obligated to an across-the-board commitment to share Co-op administrative and clerical costs.

As Psychological Services moved to a predominant role in the program and funding of the Co-op, a shift in leadership occurred, as well. Jerry Morton increasingly became the central leadership figure of the Co-op, with Bill Oakes moving to a figurehead role until his death in 1976, when Jerry Morton was officially appointed as LTVEC Director. The dominance of Psychological Services over other aspects of the Co-op was reflected in the Board's decision to maintain Jerry Morton as full-time Director of Psychological Services, and to simply tack on an additional $3,000 to that salary to cover additional responsibilities as Co-op director.

The districts began to experience benefits from membership in LTVEC, as the Co-op increasingly enjoyed a surge of renewed credibility and fiscal feasibility. In an interesting new twist, an outside intrusion (Public Law 839), in which promises by the outside agent were kept, a reciprocal relationship was shaped which benefitted the districts and thereby revitalized the Co-op. Or as Mac McDowell of Monroe County puts it, "Public Law 839 became the life-saver for financing the Co-op, but the Co-op was the life saver for the school systems."

LTVEC: CIRCA 1979

Entering the LIVEC milieu for an eighteen-day on-site visit in early March of '79, the observer was suddenly immersed into , a flowing collage of people, events, places, attitudes, dialogs, joys, disappointments, and even a few dull, empty moments—a slice in the life of an educational cooperative.

PG. 31

Through these days, the Little Tennessee Valley Cooperative was busily about its routine activities in the slightly updated locker room area of the old Everett High School gymnasium on Everett High Drive. Psychologists moved in and out of the building, took phone calls, and huddled in twos and threes to discuss special cases. Phyllis, director of the Environmental Education Project, hurried about planning an upcoming three-day retreat for project teachers and administrators. Representatives from the Co-op member school districts and other neighbor districts—Knox County, Oakridge—convened to plan for the summer Gifted Program. The Board met, talked, decided that special snow day curriculum packages would be a super idea, determined that ALOCA must maintain its administrative cost responsibilities to the Co-op, and heard Jerry's latest ideas for restructuring the budget and for developing a Handicapped Education Center. The staff met, reported problems and progress, and exchanged war stories from their schools and projects. Gynden created budgets and alternative budgets for '79-180. And Jerry provided direct leadership and support for all of these internal activities, while also communicating with TVA and other external agencies, and engaging in the yearly springtime negotiations with districts in deciding upon levels of program and budget commitments.

The purpose of the site visit had been to document a regional environment learning system, a network engaged in environmental education of some description--either formal or informal, in community or in schools. Early into the case study it became evident that LIVEC would fit no orderly or tidy definition of an environmental educational learning system. The Co-op was a network, and had to do with environmental education, but it had little in common with designed models and was, instead, a prime example of an organic, naturally occurring system.

Observations of current operations of the Co-op in light of its history, as reported in earlier pages, have therefore led the observer to make a case for LIVEC as an alternative environmental education network, one which has utility in conceptualizing the nature and evolution of net-works, and which seems also to enrich current definitions of environmental education.

PG. 32

LTVEC is a network involved directly and indirectly in environmental education of three types:

(1) The changing consciousness of the psychosocial environment.

(2) The restructuring of the political environment.

(3) The increase in individual and collective understanding of a responsibility for issues related to the physical environment.

The Psycho-Social Environment. Under Jerry Morton's leadership, promoting change in the psycho-social environment—particularly in schools, but also in the larger region--has been the primary target of the Cooperative's effort. Jerry came to the Co-op with an academic history in school psychology and a deep personal commitment to humanism and social ethics. For him, the greatest needs facing school districts and the people of the entire Little Tennessee Valley were needs for more nurturing and supportive environments, where individual needs could be met, and especially where the growing subculture of handicapped children endemic to the three-county area could begin to be remediated.

The outreach psychological services program had been the first major thrust in this direction. Psychologists first tested students for handicapping conditions, assisted in the identification of the child's needs, and participated in the planning of an individualized educational program (IEP) for each child, a program that would be essentially within the mainstream of the system's overall educational program. At the time of the case study observation, psychologists had become increasingly involved in the implementation of the IEPs and were being further utilized as consultants for special problems of teachers and administrators. Problems related to the promotion of affective growth and development of individual children, classroom climate, communications with parents, and even discipline problems now often come under the influence of the psychologists.

School districts are under constant threat of suit since the passage of state, and, later, federal laws regarding handicapped education. Note, for example, the following

PG. 33

case discussed in a recent educators' newsletter (University of Tennessee, College of Education, March, 1979):

A recent article in the Cleveland (Tennessee) Daily Banner reports a due process hearing decision involving a 14-year-old autistic child. The hearing officer reported a four-part decision as follows:

—'*That the Cleveland City School System is attempting to place Jeffrey Wade Rayburn in a special education program which is inappropriate to his condition and need.*'

—'*That the Cleveland City School System is* "denying educational services because no suitable program of education or related service is maintained."'

—'*That Walden House is an appropriate placement and that Jeffrey Rayburn should be placed at Walden House as soon as possible*'

—'*That Walden House should provide reports and all other data or procedure considerations to allow the Cleveland City School System to conduct monitoring activities as mandated by law and rules and regulations of the State Department of Education. Program must be reviewed annually.'*

Walden House is a private agency in Nashville which specializes in care for autistic children. Evidently it is the only such facility within the state. The cost to the Cleveland City School System will be $18,000 per year.

This is an example of the tremendous impact of PL 94-142 and Section 504. Some would argue that local schools cannot stand this type of expenditure. Such an argument has some validity. The argument could also be set forth that if this child could have been identified at age three and appropriate placement in the least restrictive environment started eleven years ago, that costly residential care would not now be necessary. The latter may be speculation. Nevertheless the present law is real and individuals working within the schools must be able to recognize signals and to identify handicapped conditions. Autism is a low incidence handicap; and many of us would know nothing about the cause, symptoms or required treatment.

PG. 34

It seems essential that we work diligently to incorporate appropriate material in our courses and programs so that the graduates of this College may be able to cope with even the most unusual of handicapping conditions.

~William H. Coffield, Dean.

According to Public Law 839, districts were liable if the special needs of students could not be met. Here again, the cooperative provided solutions or partial solutions to the problem. First, Jerry Morton gave the districts a language for understanding and articulating legal and programmatic responses to the needs of handicapped children. As one person interviewed described this influence, "*Jerry has brought about remarkable change in the values and attitudes of superintendents, principals, and others in the schools.*"

Still the districts had few avenues for becoming more responsive to special needs. The Co-op assisted by beginning to develop specialty programs. At the time of the site visit, in addition to regular psychological service, the Co-op had become instrumental in several additional programs which were also impacting the psycho-social environment of the region:

Handicapped Child Development Program

Class for hearing impaired

Physical therapy and speech therapy services

Program for notionally/ behaviorally disturbed gifted students

A preschool child find program for locating young handicapped children

Program for gifted youth.

Through the efforts of LTVEC, the consciousness of the districts is observably sensitive and atypically advanced in the area of affective education, and according to reports of superintendents, principals, and teachers, the psycho-social environment in schools is much improved over earlier years. In short, a language and action of caring is being spoken through the LTVEC network, as reflected in one teacher's response to the question, "What are you doing in your school?"—"*Trying to care, I guess.*"

And this plea for meaningful changes beyond schools and into the larger psycho-social community environment is being voiced more broadly, as Jerry Morton appears at hearings on the future of the Tellico Dam Project, and writes to David Freeman, the new chairman of the TVA Board:

PG. 35

While we are proud of LTVEC's record and the cooperative spirit of our communities, there is a limit to what the school systems and communities can accomplish when addressing regional Issues with local resources. LTVEC Is identifying and reaching some of those limits.The list ranges from generalized problems to detailed specifies, For example, (1) we need a centrally located Special Education Center (Vonore area), (2) we need a coordinated effort among all human service agencies to effectively serve the high incidence of adolescent pregnancies to include assistance to the surprisingly large number of young women (13 to 17 years of age) who decide to keep their babies, (3) we need to establish alternative school-type programs for the emotionally/behaviorally difficult student who is constantly being expelled or absent from school, (4) we need more effective adolescent gynecological services to cope with the diagnostic and follow -up work for the high incidence of sexual child abuse being found, (5) we need region wide planning and strategies to cope with the overcrowding of schools as a result of people moving into the area, (6) we need more comprehensive mental health services to cope with the ever Increasing emotional crises our population seems to be experiencing as a result of the pressures created by new people moving in and continual demand to change life styles at an ever Increasing rate, (7) we need region wide transportation planning to cope with the tourists, the cost of gasoline, and busing of children to school, (8) we need a regional approach to cope with the lack of or overabundance of medical services to specific communities, and (9) we need a regional approach to water usage, waste disposal, and industrial development.

The Restructuring of the Political Environment.

Networks are typically political enterprises. They are formed when smaller, individual units judge coalescence to be somehow desirable, profitable, or beneficial to their individual interests (i.e., interests in money, power, ideology, etc.). Networks, once operating, are maintained because they continue to serve the political interests of participating parties, because they are resistant to change, or because they are externally controlled.

PG. 36

The impetus to the formation of LTVEC was initially very powerful. As described earlier, two forces encouraged this coalescence: (1) the threat of impact of the model city upon the region and its school districts, and (2) the promise of money to accompany this impact. At this phase of the Co-op, however, the actual cooperative exchange was little more than shared planning. As expectations for Timberlake dwindled, another political concern replaced earlier ones--the districts became in urgent need of means to implement the Handicapped Education Law. Now real collateral entered the network exchange--to individual districts went psychological services, legal aid, and consulting; and from the districts into the maintenance of the cooperative went financial support. In addition, other services came available for very little additional cost. So for a long while, it was much a story of the fishes and the loaves. The districts gave a little, and received much.

To say that there was a cooperative educational network in existence over the past nine years is not to say that the primary mode of political activity of the various districts was a cooperative one. In fact, their investment in cooperative exchange was relatively slight, impacting less than twenty percent of their students, and for the most part, , they continued as solitary, individualistic political federations concerned with local problems, and meeting them with parochial views and solutions.

Then and now, the importance to the districts of autonomy before cooperation was realized by Jerry Morton, and clearly established as part of the LIVEC rationale. Note the following quote from a recent LTVEC proposal:

Several years ago seven school systems in Southern Appalachia decided to work together on special projects to enhance their services to children without sacrificing their individual autonomy.

It is important to note that each of the school systems had and has its own unique way of making decisions, implementing policies, and concepts about its educational goals. Their commonality lies in their desire to serve the children in the best possible way and the commitment to cooperate, when possible, with each other.

Still, formal and informal network interaction was steady over the years, and the Cooperative became a stimulus for ongoing political discussion and collective political

PG. 37

concept development related to a wide range of educational and public issues. The legal rights of children and parents; building concern and establishing local action on the question of tax base, school consolidation, career education, programs for the gifted, TVA's responsibility to the region—all entered the arena of network dialog in one form or another.

And so, in addition to an exchange of services for dollars, LIVEC was also operating to provide an opportunity for the development of a shared, sophisticated, and unified political consciousness.

On the surface the districts' continued participation in the Co-op is strictly of a utilitarian nature. According to one superintendent:

"As long as the Co-op is providing services and is cost-effective, it will be supported. When it is no longer cost effective, it won't be supported."

Still, there are indications of a deeper network operating among the seven districts, a network based on unspoken person-to-person commitments, a camaraderie built upon empathetic understandings, on shared problems, on a sense of fraternal belongingness which strengthens group cohesiveness and resists external infiltration, and on a shared admiration and trust in its leadership figure, Jerry Morton. Board members make occasional reference:

"The Co-op is a common meeting place. I begin to see the problems of Floyd P. over in Blount County and so on...Also, Bill H. I would have never known him as well as I know him now if it hadn't been for the Co-op. Now I feel freer to talk with him."

"The Co-op has encouraged my awareness of other people's questions and problems."

"It's helped me just to get with the group and share common problems. That's a big thing."

"If Jerry remains director of the Co-op, our district will stay in."

PG. 38

Thus LTVEC has contributed directly and indirectly to change in the political environment of educational systems in the region. It has been instrumental in the development of political network, has been a catalyst to the development of shared political constructs, and has concurrently contributed to an underlying personal network which brings strength, resonance and resiliency to that political network.

Current Environment Issues. Probably no other region in this nation has been more consistently engaged in what we are currently naming "environmental issues" than have the people of the Little Tennessee Valley. Their birthright to roots along the Little Tennessee River brought with it a birthright to constant impingement upon their land and way of life by external forces which claim some alien rights upon the River and its resources of energy and beauty.

Even now, a visitor to the area is left with the feeling that in the early stages of Tellico talk, the upheaval surrounding the project was radical and intense across the region, in communities, and within institutions, including school districts. People were pulled between dreams of a Camelot and dread of another Oak Ridge. In many cases deep cuts were made through the marrow of systems in which the support and direction for communities and schools were located. A high school principal in Monroe County remembers some of the difficulties:

"Well, our Lions Club was a strong organization until one of the members introduced a resolution that they were opposed to the dam. But not everyone was opposed. So that sort of destroyed our Lions Club for awhile. The same thing happened in PTA. We didn't start it back until four or five years ago. It got to a thing even your friends didn't necessarily agree with you."

The struggle, for a time, was one of survival and of maintenance of a semblance of equilibrium. It was a time of reactions, rather than initiations; of buying the TVA line rather than taking community control and self-responsibility. Even LTVEC in its inception was essentially reactive, not proactive, in regards to planning and decision-making regarding critical environmental issues.

PG. 39

Eventually the smoke screens lifted, leaving the people of the Little Tennessee Valey scarred and cynical. Now, in the spring of [19]79, the environmental issues surrounding the Tellico Project have been resurrected by the congressional decision not to close the dam. Reactions of the Co-op member school districts, however, are now more cautious and reflect the wisdom of experience:

"*Right now it's an emotional disturbance. From the beginning it was a split issue, still is a split issue. There was a loss of confidence...Most of us have adopted a wait-and-see policy—we got along without it and will get along with it. It took some of the more valuable farm lands. Has affected the roads. We have to drive buses farther to pick up children...It's kind of a no-man's-land thing now.*"

"*Now you don't hear too much about it, per se, in the community. It's sort of an attitude that people aren't going to be hurt.*"

"*It hasn't had the effect that everybody thought it would. When they started buying up farm land and moving everybody off, they just moved right out here to the other side of the community, so enrollment hasn't changed much.*"

"*It's something we read about in newspapers and see on TV. Most of the people in this area are for it at this point. Here it sits. Ninety-eight percent complete...People think it's stupid for $100 million to be sitting over there useless. The people against it in the beginning feel it makes a mockery of the court system.*"

"The Tellico Project didn't affect us. Economically, we'll lose the tax base. If it goes, we'll have people who move into the community."

Since the Tellico fiasco, among local people there has been a tendency to deny or discount environmental issues, and an active distaste for "environmentalists. "Still, the people subscribe to environmentally sound values. Jerry Morton describes this attitude:

PG. 40

"Environment is such a dirty word here. An environmentalist is a missionary who is coming in and has no idea what is going on, and says, 'You're not going to be able to earn a living because we're going to save this unique earth-worm here.' Environmentalists are outsiders. They fly in representatives from the Sierra Club who talk about flying in fishermen from Nevada, yet you know they won't arrive. Still, fundamentally these people are extremely environmentally oriented."

One modest effort toward directing this environmental orientation is the LTVEC Environmental Information and Personnel Integration Project currently funded through a grant from the Office of Environmental Education. In a recent project report, overview and goals were stated as follows:

> *The overall objective of this project is to integrate environmental information into the professional and personal lives and perceptual sets of selected high school teachers and administrators so that their individual understandings will lead them to appropriate curriculum ranges. This objective will be accomplished through a two-part effort. First, recognized experts will present environmental*

> *information to the educators. Then, through small-group strategies, the educators will be assisted in integrating this information into their own personal realities. Our hypothesis is that once the above is accomplished, the educators will initiate curriculum adjustments to teach their students the newly acquired insights as part of their normal subject matter. Through these strategies, we hope to overcome the traditional difficulty of transforming environmental information into professional and personal behaviors and ultimately to the classroom.*

PG. 41

In the project, teachers and administrators come together for Saturday workshops in which certain "experts" on current environmental issues share information through lecture, media, and discussions. In after-school follow-up sessions, a consultant with expertise in group process facilitation conducts small group follow-up, integration and extension sessions.

The sharing of information is seen as important, and certainly curriculum development is desired, as well; but the real hope of the project seems to be that it will create the beginnings of an environmental action advocacy network within the region. The project is very much an extension of philosophy and planning of Jerry Morton to increasingly engage LTVEC in meaningful involvement in the environmental issues and related regional planning. Bill Poppen, the project group process consultant, summarizes that motivation:

"He (Jerry) was concerned about the process of change and how it works in this area; how communities react to change and how change

takes place. He saw the project as training awareness raisers rather than curriculum developers."

Jerry Morton himself has said on one day to the observer:

"We hope the people in the project will move from pacifists into people who are involved. And this will serve as practice for them to extend their project experience into this new setting."

And again, on another day, to project participants:

"There is a mass of (environmental) information. Relating this information to school districts is the responsibility of these persons in the OEE grant.

You will initiate and create a process of what kinds of (environmental) planning needs to take place, and in your classrooms, what kinds of experiences need to take place for kids to do this sort of planning."

Mr. Sparks, principal of Vonore High School describes the content of those sessions consistently with other participants:

"We've hit on some things that were real informative. It's things you wouldn't think of finding out for yourself."

PG. 42

In the sessions observed, dialogue was open and active. Topics of all sorts were introduced, discussed, haggled over, laughed about, then set aside for other topics. Snatches from the discussions indicate something of the nature of the whole:

(About mass transit and new expressways.) *"That's just feeding the problem. You're talking about laying down more pavement for these cars. It's just like the world food problem—the more we feed these people, the more there will be."*

"Maryville and ALCOA don't really work together. Maryville needs the water system Alcoa has; Alcoa needs the sewage treatment system Maryville has."

"I'm gonna fill my truck up just as long as I can, and when it runs out, me and Jimmy Carter are gonna walk home."

"If unused land of Tellico were reforested, it would probably provide more energy than the dam."

"Teach them to read, write, and cipher, and work the hell out of them."

"I need to know how to work with children who come from homes that have no love."

"Ralph Nader has said our schools have more problems than they should tolerate and more solutions than they use."

Final Thoughts

The case study of the Little Tennessee Valley Educational Cooperative falls far short of providing an archetypal Regional Environmental Learning System. It does, however, seem to offer several insights into the nature of networks and networking. Observations from LTVEC and the Land Owners Organization remind us of that which we already knew--networks are little more yet nothing less

PG. 43

> than human processes, complete with all the foibles and equally replete with unlimited and immeasurable potential. Networks are observably more organic than mechanical. They are complex, non-linear, resilient, yet fragile. They have lifetimes, and must germinate and mature before becoming fully functional and productive. They demand time and space for growth and their development charts meandering pathways to strange cadences.
>
> Plastic networks, like the Charrette, cloned overnight; pressed, pushed, and artificially rewarded to produce net-work-like processes generate plastic, mechanical outcomes, and fail as networks. In sum, networks are part of the living environment, and our desire to understand, utilize, manipulate and control them brings the same gains and risks from which we have sometimes learned and too often failed to learn in painful lessons through previous experiences with control of other segments of our living environment.

I am aware of three factual errors that need correcting in the above report and possibly a fourth. On page 30, Bill Oakes's death was reported to be January 1976. He died in December 1975. I considered Bill to be a dear friend and mentor. His death was a sad moment for me. On page 31, the report identifies Phyllis (O'Donnel) as the director of the environmental grant. She was the director of the cooperative's gifted grant. John Adams was the director of the environmental grant. Page 31 also indicated that in spring of 1979 the cooperative was worried that the Alcoa City Schools would not pay its share of the cooperative's administrative costs. As I remember that time, the concern was focused on Blount County Schools.

There was talk that Blount County Schools was considering rescinding its membership from LTVEC. As the largest member school system of the cooperative, that system represented forty percent of the entire cooperative budget. If it withdrew, the question would be, could the cooperative survive? I have already reported on the shortfall in the cooperative's administrative budget for 1972. I was told some years after the fact by one of the three board of directors members that each had borrowed $10,000 to make up the $30,000 shortfall with the understanding that the delay in the grant funding coming from TVA would be provided later in the school year. On page 26 of the Stake/Brown report, it sites ARC (Appalachian Regional Commission) as the agency that was the culprit. Regrettably, whichever the funding agency was, it did not produce the missing $30,000. The cooperative had to find a way to repay those board members. It did.

As Dr. Brown was in the process of concluding her eighteen-day visit with the cooperative, she quietly told me that the principals in Blount County voiced a lot of support for the cooperative. I thanked her for the comments. I did not share that I doubted its accuracy. Most of my attention had been focused on the principals in the system who seemed to be resisting the cooperative's staff. They did not want to receive students with disabilities as I perceived the situation. Let me jump ahead in time because my current perception of the situation is not what it was in 1979.

Sometime in the early 1980s, I had a friendly conversation with a one-term superintendent from Blount County Schools. At the time, he had returned to being a principal in an elementary school near the North Carolina border. He was telling me about how it was when he started as a one-room schoolteacher in the system. Among other things, he described how he would start the potbellied stove with firewood every morning and knock a hole in ice that had formed in the water bucket the kids used for drinking water. It was simply amazing to me that the school system had changed so much during this man's lifetime. What stuck in my mind was his statement about the cooperative. He said that my big mistake was in not working more directly with the principals in the system.

I thought about that. I had been resistant to try to organize various groups within a school system. My reasoning was that the cooperative's mission was to provide the school systems with highly skilled professional service providers that would assist the systems in providing the services to their children in meeting their educational needs. The complexities of the politics within school systems in general and in rural systems in particular took generations to develop. It was highly unlikely that service providers who had not lived in the system's boundaries for a considerable period of time would gain the insights necessary to make quality inputs into the politics within their system.

An incident that reinforced this concern took place around 1980. A relatively new university professor who had moved to Blount County decided to run for the office of county executive around 1980. He was not well-known by long-time residents of the county. One Sunday afternoon while driving by a local cemetery, he noticed a large group of people by a freshly dug grave site. He got out of his car and approached the group. With sympathy in his appearance, he asked who the deceased was. After talking to a few of the grievers and expressing his regrets, he related to several mourners that he was running for the office of county executive. Then he began distributing his campaign card.

When I got into my office early the next day, Monday morning, a long-time educator in Blount County told me that everyone in the county knew what the guy had done. They were all in shock that he had disgraced himself to everyone with his insensitive behavior. He lost the election by a large margin. Offensive comments spread quickly through the community.

Sometime around the year 2010, at a social gathering, a former high school principal from Blount County Schools told me that she and several other principals had hopes that the cooperative would be successful. They were strong supports of the changes the cooperative was initiating within their system during her years as a principal. I had always valued and respected her as that high school's principal. I had no idea that she was such a strong supporter of LTVEC. I wish I had known this fact, if for no other reason than it would have made me feel better about what we were all trying to accomplish.

The overall goal of the cooperative was to be of assistance to children through the use of professional service providers within the schools. Its goal was not to become the area's dominant agency at the expense of providing quality services to children. Throughout the history of the cooperative the sharing of helpful concepts that benefited children was more important than receiving credit for those concepts or creating a superagency.

THIRTEEN
LESSONS FROM A CRISIS

The abrupt withdrawal of Blount County Schools without paying its fees created a crisis for the cooperative. As noted in the University of Illinois' 1979 study of the LTVEC, that a system would withdraw from the cooperative was a matter of concern. You may recall that the Stake/Brown study misidentified the school system. It named the potentially withdrawing system as Alcoa. The actual system was Blount County Schools.

Around March 1980, the Blount County School System gave a full school year's notice that it would terminate its membership with LTVEC as of June 30, 1981. A full school year's notice to withdraw was required as stated in the membership contract with LTVEC. For example, if a system decided to end its membership in January of the 1910-1911 school year, then it would remain a member of the co-op through the rest of that school year and through the 1911-1912 school year. A school year was defined as from the first of July through the thirtieth of June. During the full year of notification, that system would pay all fees and expenses that had been its commitment to the cooperative.

Those expenses included its membership fee and all of the

charges for services the cooperative was providing to it. The reason for this stipulation was that the other member school systems would have time to make whatever adjustments were necessary to maintain the financial stability of LTVEC. Blount County Schools was the largest member system with forty percent of the total members' student population. The system had contracted for about forty percent of the psychological and special education services the cooperative was providing to its member systems.

The charges to Blount County Schools for the services it was receiving from the cooperative were in the range of one hundred thousand dollars. That money paid the salaries of the professionals delivering their services to the system as well as the needed support costs. In preparing the budget for the 1982-1983 school year, it would be a simple enough task to eliminate the cost of those services since the school system had terminated them. That left only the co-op expenses paid from the system's membership fee of thirteen thousand dollars to be dealt with.

The agreement for LTVEC membership held that if the members decided to terminate the cooperative as an organization, the member systems would divide the assets of the cooperative between them on the basis of the percentage of students each system had of their combined student populations. If one or more school systems left the cooperative, but the cooperative continued as an organization, those systems leaving the cooperative forfeited their rights to any of the assets of LTVEC. The downside of this agreement was that if the cooperative's deficits were greater than its assets, then the remaining members of the organization would divide up their share of the deficit in the same manner set up for the assets.

Without this contract agreement, if a run of member systems declared their withdrawal from the co-op, then the last system to announce its withdrawal would be the one stuck with having to pay all of the cooperative's unpaid bills. That was a big reason for requiring the full school year notice to withdraw. It was protection for all the member systems. The remaining systems would have a full year to be able to make adjustments in covering the lost revenue created by a system's withdrawal.

The problem for the cooperative and Blount County Schools was that around March of 1981, Blount County announced that it was not going to withdraw from the cooperative after all. It would be a full member of the cooperative the next year, the 1981-1982 school year. Then around April or May of 1982, the system announced that as of June 30, 1982, it would no longer be a member of the cooperative. The cooperative's board of directors stated that the school system was required to give the co-op a full school year's notice of withdrawal. The earliest the school system could withdraw its membership would be June 30, 1983. The system disagreed. It stated that it gave LTVEC a year's notice of withdrawal back in the spring of 1980 and that notice was still in effect. As of June 30, the system would not pay its membership for the 1982-1983 school year, nor would it have any contracts for services with the cooperative.

Immediate adjustments for the cooperative had to be made. That meant informing the school psychology service providers and various therapists of the current year that the cooperative did not have a contract with Blount County Schools for their services in the coming school year, so it could not employ them for the next year. A few full-time school psychologists were working in the system through the cooperative at that time as well as some graduate assistants and part-time speech and physical therapists. We assured them that we would assist them in every way we could to be of service to them in obtaining employment.

The shock to the professionals serving in Blount County Schools in losing their employment within a month or two was mitigated by the school system's offering to hire all of the professional service providers employed by the cooperative to become the school system's employees. Once again, the issue was never the quality of the service the cooperative's professionals provided. The issue was control of those professionals. Some of the cooperative's staff did accept those job offers while others chose to go elsewhere. The administrative staff of the co-op did all it could to support the individuals affected by the Blount County School System's action. Several of the co-op's member systems increased their contracts with the cooperative so that those professionals released by the Blount system could work in their systems. These professionals were highly regarded.

Balancing LTVEC's budget for the 1982-1983 school year within a month or so of the start of that year was simplified because of the way it maintained its monthly records to ensure that every system received the exact services it was paying for plus the co-op's relatively low administrative costs. As a result, the money that would have been paid to the terminated service providers matched the lost revenue for services and the related support costs.

The thirteen thousand dollars that the Blount County School System was paying as its membership fee presented a more difficult problem. The bookkeeper and I were able to find ways of reducing the generalized expenses of maintaining the cooperative's existence by nine thousand dollars without hurting the organization. This left four thousand dollars that needed to be cut from the coming year's budget. Every solution to reduce the budget by the required four thousand dollars put the very existence of the cooperative at risk. I had just a month and a few days to find a solution that would work. I found it.

I would reduce my work week of forty hours a week to thirty hours a week. That reduced my annual salary by three thousand dollars and the related support costs by a thousand dollars. I needed to work thirty hours a week in order to remain in the teacher retirement system as a full-time employee. I felt confident that various school systems, non-profit organizations and the university would want to contract for some of my time along with other surprise opportunities. They would establish a contract with the cooperative for me to accomplish various tasks. Time proved I was correct.

The cooperative's board of directors adopted the amended budget as I had proposed it with my salaried work week consisting of thirty hours a week. The board also insisted that it sue Blount

County Schools for breach of contract and the system be ordered to pay the thirteen thousand dollars it owed the cooperative. Several of the board members were most insistent that the co-op recover the thirteen thousand dollars the school system owed LTVEC. They were quite confident that LTVEC would win its case. The Blount County School System was clearly breaking its contract with the co-op. The board voted to sue Blount County Schools for the thirteen thousand dollars they were under contract to pay during the 1982-1983 school year.

I vigorously argued with the board not to sue Blount County Schools. I was the only one who was directly affected, and I thought, correctly, enough contracts with other organizations for my professional services would make up for the lost salary. One of the purposes of the cooperative was to promote cooperation between school systems. If the board was to sue Blount County Schools, it didn't make any difference if the cooperative won or lost the court case. Key citizens of Blount County would remember that the co-op sued the county for generations to come. They would have bad feelings about the cooperative. Blount County Schools would probably never rejoin the cooperative if they did this. The board was adamant. They had to sue the school system to protect the cooperative from other member systems dropping out on a moment's notice, leaving the remaining few having to pay the accumulated financial obligations created by the many.

How did this crisis arise? Why did Blount County School System announce that it was withdrawing from the cooperative, change its mind and then change it again? The explanations reveal many of the struggles the cooperative faced throughout its early history.

When Blount County Schools generously offered to house the cooperative's central offices in the old Everett High School complex, the high school building had been converted to serve children with serious disabilities between the ages of six and eighteen years. Another building on the campus had been a multilevel gymnasium. In 1976, the cooperative occupied the main level of the gymnasium building for office space. The director's office and the accountant/office manager's offices were located there as well as offices for the cooperative's service providers. In the basement level of the building the cooperative's early childhood program for four-to-six-year-old children with special needs was located. That program was funded by Blount County Schools. Over a few years it evolved into a program for birth-to-three-year-old children. The cooperative had been awarded a federal grant to operate the birth-to-three-year-old program. The county school system continued to fund the four-to-six-year-old program under its management system while the cooperative focused its attention on the birth-to-three program.

The federal grant provided funding to establish the Birth-to-Three program for children with disabilities in the three counties of the cooperative, Blount, Loudon and Monroe. The three sites utilized the services of a school psychologist, several specialty therapists (speech, physical and occupational therapists) as well as both a vision mobility specialist and a preschool special education teacher.

The Blount County Birth-to-Three program continued to be located in the old Everett High School gymnasium building.

While the cooperative was still operating the Blount County four-to-six-year-old program for children with disabilities, several of the cooperative's professional staff also provided services to students in the system's special education center for the county's older children. Across the street from the gymnasium building was a county agency's program for a daycare type of operation that included services to children with disabilities.

Difficulties between the cooperative's service providers and the staff of the daycare center developed. The core issue revolved around the center's failure to provide the four-to-six-year-old children with special needs the services mandated by the special education laws.

Difficulties between the cooperative's service providers and the staff of the private daycare developed over time. The core issue revolved around the preschool daycare center's failure to provide children with special needs the services mandated by the special education laws.

The daycare center was claiming that they were providing the special needs children with services that met the requirements of the special education laws. From the cooperative's staff perspective, they were not. There was no question that the center was providing the children with caring attention, but they were not meeting the individualized educational needs of the children. Appropriate educational strategies for each child were lacking and no apparent evaluations of the children's progress in meeting educational progress were made. A number of other violations were present as well. As a result, parents of some of those children decided to remove their children from the daycare center and into the cooperative's early childhood program.

This angered the director of the daycare program. She was a highly regarded member of the community in that county. She created one of the few daycare programs that would accept children with disabilities long before the special education laws were written. In that regard she was an outstanding pioneer. Her opinion of the cooperative's program was low. What seemed to matter to many in the larger community was that they admired the service the daycare center provided to the community and resented any criticism of it. The tension between the two organizations grew to the point that a few of the parents within that program filed for a due process hearing against the cooperative's preschool program. They charged that the program the cooperative managed for four-to-six-year-olds' special needs was not providing those children the services they needed.

During the hearing, which was an open hearing, the cooperative had the opportunity to present its program to the hearing officer. Under oath, the various therapists described their evaluation process of the children in question, what their intervention strategies were, how those strategies were integrated to provide support for the strategies of the other intervention specialists, how they were evaluating the success of their interventions and adjusting those interventions when the data warranted such adjustments.

I had counseled all of the staff who were scheduled to testify that they always tell the truth. They were to be careful not to speculate beyond the bounds of the data they had to support their testimony. It was perfectly all right to simply say that they did not know the answer to a question if they did not know it. That answer would simply reflect that they stayed within the bounds of their professional knowledge.

Since the hearing was an open one, visitors could listen to the entire process. Several school administrators attended the hearing, including some from member systems of the cooperative. Those testifying were excluded from being in the listening audience of the hearing. That practice was to prevent the possibility of collusion between witnesses in providing supportive statements to difficult questions.

I was proud of the presentation of the co-op's preschool individualized education program for its children with disabilities. After the hearing had ended and visitors were leaving, I asked one superintendent what he thought of the cooperative's program. His answer surprised me. He said, "That's an expensive program." His response reminded me of the pressure all public-school administrators are under when a law demands they provide services without fully providing the funds to do so. If they don't provide the required services, they will be legally accountable. If they can't balance their operating budgets, their school boards will fire them. If they take money from existing educational programs in their school system to provide the required special education services, their principals and teachers will raise significant protests which could cause their school board to remove them. School system superintendents earn their salaries.

During the time of conflict with the preschool program, a conflict between the co-op staff and the school system's special education school for their older students was developing. The conflict revolved around the cooperative's service providers' attempts to assist the school's staff to more appropriately address the educational needs of their students. The co-op staff reported that appropriate individualized education plans (IEP) for every child were lacking. This and other related concerns were brought up to the teachers and the school principal. These issues were raised in as diplomatic a way as possible by the co-op staff as far as I could tell. Many of the shortcomings were reportedly supported by monitoring visits from the state department of education. The monitors were able to identify weaknesses in the school's records and order them corrected. It was rumored that one child's written IEP had been reused for several years after the year it had been approved by the state monitors. A monitor finally noticed that the only thing changed on the student's progress report was the date. Whether or not this was true, it reflects the concerns about the overall educational programs being presented to the children and concerns about their individual educational plans (IEP's).

The co-op staff was able to work with a medical researcher who was doing research in teaching children who were so seriously disabled that they were confined to a wheelchair, lacked any communication skills, could not feed themselves or control their biological functions. They were able to engage him to work with such a child. The cooperative staff had indications that this adolescent girl's mental functioning was relatively high. Her mind seemed to be trapped inside a body that it could not control. She couldn't do much more than move her head around so that she could see in different directions. The student's parents, the school's administrator and the child's primary teacher agreed to match her with the researcher.

The medical researcher was doing pioneering research of that time. With the assistance of the staff at the school and the cooperative, he was attempting to do something like attaching a pointer to the student's head and teaching her to move the pointer around to press the keys and/or pictures on a computer screen. Once she had learned to do that, he would try to teach her to type out words. The student accomplished the task to the point that she was typing in complete sentences, it was reported. What she communicated caused major changes to take place both at school and in her home environment.

Despite this outcome and some other positive developments, the lack of full implementation of the requirements of the special education laws in the special education center were such that the cooperative's staff requested a meeting with the system's superintendent and key supervisors. A meeting was arranged. The staff made its report. At its conclusion, the staff was asked to leave the meeting while I was requested to remain. After they left, the superintendent stated that it was not good for employees to be present when the administration was making decisions about what to do about a situation.

That was not how the cooperative functioned. Those involved in a situation were a part of the decision-making team. However, that was how this system was functioning at that time. The supervisor present at the meeting said to me, "We practice the policy that if we don't have something good to say about someone, we don't say anything." That comment was an indication of the rest of the discussion. It ended by the superintendent saying his system would look into the concerns. The co-op staff continued to provide some services in that special education center for the rest of the year. Those services were provided from other sources the next year.

In the fall of 1979, three Blount County Schools officials, the supervisor of special education, a more senior supervisor and a junior high school principal made an urgent request to meet with me. This was highly unusual. The principal had been highly critical of the cooperative and a leader in calling for the system to just leave the co-op. They clearly had a problem. When we met, the special education supervisor stated that they had a mother of a blind dwarf child who was insisting that her child return from the Tennessee School for the Blind in Nashville and attend regular junior high school. The mother said that her son complained that he already knew everything they were teaching in his classes at the school for the blind. He was bored. He wanted to come home and go to school at the junior high school he would normally attend. That was it. She was bringing him home and the junior high school would have to take him. They told her she would have to wait for them to work out the details. She said there was no need to wait. He was coming home. What did I think they should do?

I knew the unquestionable reality of the state and federal special education laws was that the school system would have to evaluate the child to determine if he qualified as a special needs child that could not receive an appropriate education without modified educational assistance. The school system and the junior high school principal would not like my recommendations to them. I was correct. They were certain that a normal educational setting, a regular junior high school, was not the proper place for this child. I explained that if the mother wanted to bring a due process hearing against the school system for refusing to evaluate the child and to develop an appropriate educational plan for the child, they would lose the case. It was that simple. No matter what the system did to avoid evaluating the child and developing an educational plan to meet the child's needs, in the end, the system would have to do it.

Okay, the system agreed. They wanted one of the cooperative's school psychologists or a school psychology doctoral intern at the cooperative to do an intellectual evaluation of the child. I was unsure that the cooperative had anyone who was trained to test a blind child's intellectual abilities. I asked them for a day's time to see if we had an appropriately trained professional to conduct the evaluation. The next day I met with the supervisors to report that the educational cooperative did not have a school psychologist who had been trained to conduct such an evaluation. I did not know of any area psychologists who were qualified for such an evaluation.

"Well, what should we do?" they asked.

My suggestion was that I could do the verbal portion of an individual intelligence test as a screening measure to see how he scored on individual subtests in the verbal section as well as to obtain a composite score in verbal IQ. Of course, I could not administer the performance half of the intelligence test, as he could not see what he was to do on that section. That section required him to respond visually to the testing tasks. The results of the verbal testing might give the school system some clues as to the intellectual functioning of the child providing guidance for developing strategies in how to proceed in this case. They agreed. The testing date was established.

After I had tested the child, I made my report to the school system. This child, this blind child of very short stature, produced test results that found the child to have a verbal IQ in the highly gifted range as defined by the Tennessee Department of Education's Rules and Regulations for identifying gifted students. I explained to the school system that without the performance portion of the intelligence test being administered to a child, they could not use my test results to declare the child intellectually gifted. However, it was clear to me that they would be in legal jeopardy if they did not determine to place the child in the junior high school as the mother had requested. They would have to continue their professional efforts to determine how the child's disabilities would interfere with the child's ability to receive a normal public-school education and make the appropriate adjustments. I went on to report that during the testing process, the child was highly articulate and eager to please me. He was very courteous and pleasant to interact with. I thought he had the social skills to interact well with other children and adults.

The system's representatives were not overly pleased with my results. The junior high school principal's body language indicated that he was "agitated" by my comments. The officials thanked me for the recommendations, indicating that they would handle the situation from then on.

That was it. I was never informed as to what was decided about the child. I did not know if an individualized educational plan had been developed for the child or if he had been allowed to attend his home junior high school.

Several months after providing the school system with my oral and written report, I was attending a regional conference for school principals and supervisors. Walking into a small session group a little late, I was surprised to see the junior high school principal who was considering admitting the blind child into his school. He was commenting to the group about a blind dwarf child.

As best that I can remember, the principal said something like, 'He was such a delight to have in my school. I was so worried about his being in the school with all of the students. When classes would change, in all of that rushing chaos, I was afraid he would be knocked down and hurt. We assigned a football player to be with him at all times during the out-of-classroom time to protect him. The boy was so appreciative of everything anyone did for him that everyone came to like him. The football players quickly adopted him. They let it be known that he was under their protection. Our school adopted him. We all look out for him; students, teachers, staff, all of us. He is such an addition to our school. And the teachers said he knew all of the classroom material. He was up to date in every class. They agreed that he was gifted. The only problem that came up was that the boy sometimes became dehydrated towards the end of the day. He was too short to get a drink from the water fountains. He didn't want to cause anyone any kind of inconvenience, so he never asked for help getting up to the waterspout for a drink. Well, as soon as we found out about that, I had the woodworking shop make steps for every water fountain in the school. We weren't going to let this continue. This boy is such a nice person. Admitting this child into our school was the best thing we could have done.'

That junior high school principal became one of the educational cooperative's strongest supporters. He retired at the end of that school year, became an elected school board member and was appointed to represent the school board on LTVEC's board of directors. He was the force behind the decision of Blount County Schools to announce around May of 1982, that they were not withdrawing from the cooperative as of June 30, 1983. Sometime before May of 1983, this person died. Shortly after his death, Blount County Schools announced that it was withdrawing from LTVEC effective June 30, 1983, and would not pay its dues for the 1983-1984 school year. As stated above, the LTVEC Board of Directors declared that was a violation of the contract the system had agreed to. This conflict led to LTVEC filing suit against the school system.

As an aside, I met with the student in question about five years ago. He gave his permission for me to share this story. He had gotten a college degree and taken several graduate courses in psychology. He did not remember my testing him. He did remember the school psychologist who worked with him when he arrived at the junior high school. His memory of that school psychologist was very positive as was his entire experience in the Blount County School system.

An attorney for one of the cooperative's school systems donated his service to represent the cooperative in taking the suit against Blount County Schools to court. Close to a year passed before the case was to be heard in court. The co-op's suit was to recover the thirteen thousand dollars. The attorney accompanied me when I was providing a deposition for the court with the Blount County Schools' superintendent and his attorney cross-examining me. On the day of the court case, we all walked into the courthouse and approached the chamber of the hearing when the LTVEC attorney stopped us. He said that Blount County Schools wanted to settle the case for nine thousand dollars. He went on to explain the reason that was acceptable. Even if we won the case, we would have to pay the court costs which would be about four thousand dollars. Either way, the co-op was only going to receive nine thousand dollars.

I checked with the superintendent of Sweetwater City Schools, Joe Sherlin, who was with us at the courthouse. He agreed that it was best for us to settle. The Blount County School system never rejoined the cooperative. A year later the Maryville School System withdrew its membership with the co-op after paying all its fees. When I met with that superintendent to ask what the cooperative had done to make him dissatisfied with its service, he smiled and said that everything was fine. He noted that a few years before, they had hired the cooperative's special education consultant as their supervisor of special education, and they planned to hire the cooperative's school psychologist for the next year. The cooperative had done well by his system. It was just that there was a sense of solidarity with the Blount County School System. Maryville was simply a part of Blount County and needed to maintain cordial relations with the county decision makers.

As I have noted, I was able to obtain contracts for my professional services that made up for my reduced salary. That remained true for the rest of my career with the cooperative.

FOURTEEN
YEARS BEYOND THE CRISIS

The cooperative was able to continue functioning after the withdrawal of Blount County Schools and Maryville City Schools. I was able to recover the lost three thousand dollars of my salary when Blount County withdrew in the first year of their absence. That recovery remained constant until my retirement. In essence, I never reduced my workweek hours. I was always so busy that only once was I able to use the full month of retirement I earned as a full-time, twelve-month employee. That perk was in the contract with the cooperative as worked out by Bill Oakes. I speculate that he set that up as a result of the contract he had with the University of Tennessee before he was involved in the creation of the cooperative. The contract allowed one to accumulate unused vacation days from year to year. By the mid 1980's, I had accumulated so many vacation days that the system's auditors pointed out to the board of directors that if I died, my heirs would want to be paid for the unused vacation days. That would bankrupt the cooperative. It simply did not have the funds to cover that expense. The board gave me one year to use all of those vacation days and then I would lose them. Thereafter, vacation day accumulations could be no more than thirty regardless of how many had not been used. The workload was such that I was never able to take full benefit of the vacation days allowed me.

Looking back on the Blount County School System situation, it allowed the cooperative to be much more flexible in the kind of services it would create or improve upon for the benefit of the area's children. That does not mean that the cooperative became an organization of thousands of members. Its size remained relatively small until recent years. The impact of its ideas was what counted. That impact was large even when the ideas failed to be fully implemented. Remember, the goal of the cooperative has always been to find ways to better serve children without interfering in the operational issues of the cooperating school systems. Here are some examples of those efforts.

The Birth-to-Three program for children with disabilities has already been mentioned. From the beginning of the cooperative's early childhood program into its evolution into the Birth-to-Three program there was one constant force, Pam Potocik. The school psychologist, Pam Potocik, provided the critical leadership that enabled the program to deliver superior early childhood educational services to these children. Her leadership carried the program through decades of changes in funding patterns and shifts in policy focus at local, state and federal levels.

When the cooperative had to leave the free office and classroom space provided by Blount County Schools, it relocated the Birth-to-Three program of Blount County to space provided by the Lutheran Church of Maryville. After a few years, that program site relocated to a commercial building and remained there for several years. The Birth-to-Three Program had three program sites. Blount County's site was the largest one. The Loudon site was located in the Lenoir City/Loudon Vocational Center. The Monroe County site was ultimately consolidated with the Loudon County site due to funding issues. The area school systems did not provide funding for the Birth-to-Three program because that age group was not included in the special education laws. When a child was about to turn four years old, transition meetings with the child's school system's four-through-six-year-olds special education program staff took place. After the preschool grants had expired, funding from the state's department of education as well as donations from the cooperative's board of directors, Blount County, Loudon County United Way and individual donations allowed the Birth-to-Three Program to continue.

The school systems were required, by law, to create programs for preschool children four through five years of age. All of the systems' supervisors of education knew that services provided to the birth to three-year-olds were a clear money saver. Special service programs for this age group brought about so much improvement in the actual functioning of the children that they did not require as intensive a level of services when they turned three as compared to others who had not been in a comparable program.

The Birth-to-Three program was a combination of two innovative strategies. While demonstrating the value of the integrated services delivery model, its system of integrating various activities of the program into a cohesive unit while enabling the staff to maintain each child's individualized educational program was remarkable. Kathy Russell, lead teacher in the Maryville Birth-to-Three program, compiled a book of the integrated activities that also included sample IEPs used in the program to ensure that every child's individualized needs were met. The book, *Kids are Kids,* was published by LTVEC and used by early education programs across the country. A national church organization recommended it to all of its preschool programs.

The integrated activities were critical in managing the interests of the wide range of ages, development, and different disabilities such as that population presents. A vision and hearing impaired six-month-old, a cognitively bright, eighteen-month-old child who is confined to a wheelchair and an intellectually challenged thirty-month-old child could all be among the children attending the program. It took a carefully planned strategy in order to have each day be a well-organized and protective learning environment for every child. Naturally, these children required the presence of highly specialized professionals throughout their time in the center. The ratio of adult to child was almost always one to one. The safety and emotional well-being of the children were of prime importance.

There was a lead teacher and as many aides as were required along with a wide variety of professional service providers. On a given morning there might be seven or eight children with disabilities in the classroom. The coordination of the professional service providers working with specific children and maintaining a cohesive classroom structure was a challenge. The *Kids are Kids* book very carefully explained how these challenges were met. It is not realistic in this format to provide the reader with a detailed explanation of the strategies used. Perhaps a brief description will serve to motivate those interested parties to explore the strategies in greater detail.

The months of the year were divided into twelve themes. The theme for September was the color red and things that go. The toys available for the children to use would all have the color red in them. The toys would all be the things that move like a car, a train, a bicycle, etc. The speech therapist would tie "R" sounds into her therapy, the physical therapist would have red Post-it notes with train tracks drawn on them for a child to put together so that he could push the red train engine on it, the occupational therapist would have a red ball for a child to bounce on the floor, the vision mobility specialist would use as many "R" words as possible in providing assistance to her student. By each service provider's station in the classroom, the child's IEP would be posted. The IEP indicated the specific objectives a child being worked with had recently achieved, partially achieved and the next developmentally appropriate objectives to be accomplished.

Even when the six-month-old child needed a diaper changed, there would be the IEP objectives posted at the changing station for that child. For example, if the physical therapist was working on having the child reach for an object, the staff person changing the diaper would be swinging an attractive object in the air above the child to stimulate her reaching for it as a way of holding the child's attention while the diaper was changed. At snack time the teacher would have red things to eat. After the children's caregivers had arrived and left around one in the afternoon, the classroom staff and professional service providers would meet and discuss the progress of every child and review the IEP goals and objectives to include the focus objective for the next session with the child.

This process was so effective under the leadership of the program's coordinator, Pam Potocik, that it received the 1987 National Exemplary Program Award in Early Childhood Intervention from the American Council in Rural Special Education at a conference in Bellingham, Washington. Three papers on programs conducted by LTVEC were presented at the Innovative Programs, Research and Technologies in Rural Education conference in Bellingham. The result of a carefully conducted study of the measurable improvements the Birth-to-Three Program produced in the children with disabilities titled, "Cooperative Professional Services for Severely Handicapped Children in Rural Areas: Implementation of Progress and Analysis of Child Progress Data" provided clear proof of the importance of this program.

With supportive funding from the state, the Birth-to-Three Program was both a center-based and parent-support-based program. The parent-based component of the program allowed professional service providers to make home visits to provide specific suggestions to the parents of young children with disabilities. As the years progressed, the state funding shifted from support of center-based programming to home-based programming. Eventually, the center-based programs lost all of their financial support. Fortunately, the strength of the cooperative's home-based program's success was such that the state is currently funding LTVEC's expanded home-based program in Blount, Loudon and Monroe Counties.

The two other papers presented at the Bellingham, Washington, conference provide some insights as to the range of the cooperative's activities in the mid 1980s. "Career Training: Strategies for Training

Disadvantaged Rural Youth" documented the strategies used to help high school students attending vocational school who were identified as likely dropouts to stay in school and graduate from high school or get a GED. Dr. Leona Motes was the project director. Students in one system's vocational school who were receiving the intervention strategies were compared to a matched set of students in another system's vocational school who were not receiving the intervention strategies. All of the students in the study were living in poverty situations, were failing in school and had high absentee rates. This project was funded through a three-year grant. The students receiving the program's services were successful in several tracked categories. One tracking category was the percentage of students who had graduated or passed the GED. Ninety-seven percent of the students receiving the support services had graduated or passed the GED. The students who did not receive the services had a much poorer record. Thirty percent of those students had dropped out of school. This group of students had even lower results in other tracking categories used by the project.

Three major components to the intervention strategies were used in this project. One component was having the students attend a class focused on preparations for employment that met once a week. The second component was tied closely to the first one. To combat the chronic absenteeism of the students, the second component was the highly successful strategy of paying the students one dollar for coming to school for the class. The third component provided each student with one hour of consultation with a school psychologist.

The organization providing the grant for this project discontinued the one hour of consultation with a school psychologist after the first year. The organization's grant administrator felt that one hour a week of consultation with a school psychologist was not enough to make a significant difference in a student's overall performance. The cooperative staff did not agree with this decision and presented evidence to support their position. It did not cause the decision to be reversed.

The funding organization's administrator also had difficulty in thinking that paying the students one dollar for attending class was the right thing to do. He considered a dollar per class not to be enough to cause the students to attend the class. His reasoning was that the money was a hollow bribing of the students and therefore a waste of taxpayer money. However, the grant continued to provide the funds to pay this component.

A point of confusion concerned the selection of the students to participate in the project. The cooperative's staff thought one thing and the organization's administrator's understanding was much more extensive than what the cooperative's staff understood it to be. Technically, none of the students selected met the grant's requirements. While the selected students might have met the more rigorous requirements if they had been applied, they had not been. The grant was discontinued.

The organization's administrator understood that the cooperative had not purposely misunderstood the requirement for selecting the students and did not want to cause undue harm to the cooperative other than to discontinue the grant. His understanding was greatly appreciated. It was pointed out that the grant's activities did produce significant improvements in the students who participated in it. The administrator agreed but continued to give the impression that the payment to the students of one dollar to attend the class once a week was a waste of money and inappropriate.

I bring this misunderstanding and disagreement about the one dollar a week payment and one hour a week of meeting with a school psychologist to emphasize that when it appears that a program to assist children seems to have failed, it may not have. As time passes, there may be indications that the concepts of a program may have survived and become accepted.

In this case, something very positive took place that demonstrated that the long-term impact of a good program that did not continue did take place. Several months after this project's funding had been discontinued, a program on a local TV station scheduled a discussion addressing the high rate of school dropouts in the region and strategies on how to reduce that rate. A panel of community leaders would address the issues. Those leaders were from various government and community agencies such as the state mental health agency, the university, area colleges and the human services organizations.

I tuned into the evening program just as the panel members were being introduced. About fifteen of them were sitting in three tiered rows of chairs. To my surprise, the grant administrator of our vocational school dropout project sat in nearly the last seat of the third row. He was the one who thought that paying students a dollar to attend a class was just not the right thing to do.

Since he was seated towards the end of the last row, the TV program's moderators did not get to him until shortly before the conclusion of the program. At last, they asked him what his thoughts were on helping students stay in school. His response was something like this, "These potential dropouts are usually very poor. It's hard for them to meet their basic needs. I say we pay them a little, something like a dollar each day they attend school. That's not much money to us, but it's really meaningful to these students. They will stay in school for that. We can't afford to let them drop out. A dollar a day is a real bargain for society as a whole."

The cooperative's vocational school dropout prevention program was a true service to the students who participated in it, and it was a success in assisting a major organization to understand the issues and consider implementing positive strategies to address the problem. The cooperative's role has always been one of assisting our children. The cooperative does not have to be the exclusive agency in controlling the strategies and the understandings of others. The cooperative shares what it learns so that others can continue to spread that knowledge. That way we all gain.

The third paper presented at the Bellingham conference focused on a theme that has been discussed earlier. You will recognize that theme through the title of the paper, "Recruitment, Employment and

Retention of High-Tech Professional Special Education Staff in Rural Settings Through Management that Stresses Emotional Well-Being."

Grant writing became a revenue source for the cooperative in the 1980s and 90s. Some grant projects that quickly come to mind include writing grants to the state's department of education's family resource center initiative on behalf of school systems. The first such grant was for Lenoir City Schools. It focused on supporting parental involvement in early educational activities with the school system. Lenoir City Schools carefully selected a board of directors that included several parents to guide the cooperative in writing the grant. It was funded and continues to successfully function today.

Another grant written for Lenoir City Schools was to Monterey Mushrooms, which had a large mushroom growing operation near Lenoir City and employed many Latin Americans. The mushroom firm had experienced difficulty employing local citizens in their plant because of their method of payment. The plant paid on the total amount of mushrooms picked per day. It was possible for a first-year employee to make a very competitive wage compared to working for other businesses in the area.

Since the amount of the daily reimbursement was based upon the quantity of mushrooms picked during the workday, taking frequent cigarette breaks, coffee breaks, telephone calls, long lunch sessions, and just experiencing downtime took away time for picking mushrooms. The Latin Americans had a different orientation to the work ethic. They were more oriented to working without many interruptions in their on-the-job time. As a result, the Latin Americans made a good amount of money per day while those from the local area did not.

Monterey Mushrooms found it beneficial to assist Latin Americans to enter the country legally, obtain appropriate work permits and relocate their families to live near their facilities. The downside of the plant's efforts was the fact that a lot of children lacking English communication skills were entering the Lenoir City

Schools. The school system needed assistance in its efforts to integrate these children successfully. The grant was for ten thousand dollars that would be spent towards employing an educator specifically trained to assist the children in the use of English. Monterey Mushrooms funded the grant. I was told that the grant amount awarded was the largest grant the corporation had ever provided a school system. Lenoir City Schools became a leader in integrating English-as a-second-language students into the regular school program.

Based upon the success of the Lenoir City Schools Family Resource Center, the Loudon County School System contracted with the cooperative to write a Family Resource Center grant for their system. The grant was funded. It was written with a focus on preschool issues.

The cooperative assisted a preschool teacher in Monroe County Schools to write a grant to the U. S. Office of Education. The co-op was particularly helpful in developing the budget of the proposal, allowing the creative concepts of the teacher to be communicated clearly to the granting agency. The grant required the system's superintendent to approve and sign the proposal. It would be funded for five years. To promote the continuation of the grant- funded activities beyond the five years of funding, the grant required the school system to produce a pledge to spend fifty thousand dollars a year in cash or in-kind contributions for its preschool program after the grant had expired. The superintendent approved the proposal and signed it.

A few months later, it was announced that the system had been awarded the grant. This was a significant honor to the school system as the granting agency had received an unusually high number of applicants and could only fund a very few of them. The superintendent stated that the system would not accept the grant. He felt that he could not in good faith commit the school system to having to put up fifty thousand dollars a year to continue its preschool initiative once the funding period had expired. Even after I explained that they did not have to put the actual fifty thousand dollars into their preschool program after five years but could count in-kind expenditures as part or all of the fifty thousand dollars, the superintendent was adamant. He could not commit that kind of money to come from the school system. It was just too big a commitment to his community.

I called Washington, D. C. and spoke to the director of the funding agency that provided the grant. She assured me that the system was already putting in at least fifty thousand dollars of in-kind funds to support its preschool program. All of those funds could be counted as the fifty thousand dollars requirement of continuation contributions to the system's preschool grant obligations. She went on to say that they had been funding this grant project for more than ten years. To the best of her knowledge not one of the grant recipients had put in any cash to meet the grant's requirement of continuation funds after the grant ended. All of the other systems had used in-kind funds to meet that requirement. I explained all of this to the superintendent. He did not change his mind. He could not commit his system to come up with that much money five years into the future.

The preschool teacher, the author of the grant, was very disappointed. At the end of the school year, she resigned her position and was hired by a nearby school system. That system liked her grant proposal, adopted it and made the author/teacher the director of the project. Children received the benefit of her work and the cooperative's work in assisting the teacher to write the grant. The children receiving the new services were not the ones that we all thought would be the beneficiaries, but children in the region did benefit. We, as professional educators, share our ideas. We do that at conferences, among fellow professionals and in our social settings. Good ideas in education tend to be passed on to others. They survive the tenure of appointed officials.

It is important to value the resisting superintendent for his efforts to protect the financial well-being of the citizens he serves. He understands the needs, finances and other important issues of the community he serves far better than I do. For reasons I never understood, this superintendent may well have made the best decision for his community at that time. I valued the superintendent for his honesty and steady desire to serve children. When we had an opportunity to be together at professional gatherings, co-op board meetings and the like, he always made a point to praise the cooperative and its contributions to his school system.

As the early years of the cooperative passed, the school systems began hiring their own full-time school psychologists. The time came when the cooperative did not employ any. Even the school psychology interns became unavailable. That happened because of the changes in the nation's licensing laws concerning internship requirements for becoming doctoral level school psychologists. Without going into great detail, the internship requirements became far more expensive in both time and money for school systems to provide an accredited internship in partnership with the interns' training institutions.

In December 1985, the non-profit organization operating the Knoxville Alternative Center for Learning, the region's alternative school, contracted with the cooperative for me to become ACL's director on a half-time basis. The organization's founding director was resigning his half-time position as ACL's director and as a university professor to become a full-time principal in a nearby school system's elementary school. The ACL program had accumulated a reserve fund to cover funding losses from grants and various participating school systems. The program's funding from grants had come to an end, and the support from some school systems was ending. The task for me was either to save the program, build it up to such an extent that one of the supporting school systems would take over the operation of ACL or to prove to the educational community that the strategies used by the ACL were worthy of replication after the ACL had ceased to exist.

Before my arrival as the director of the alternative school, the program was one of strict rules and consequences. It was reported that the students were not allowed to speak or communicate with each other while in class. The teachers were not allowed to sit down when the students were in attendance. They were required to walk up and down the classroom aisles in order to better catch students passing notes to each other. Perhaps the contrast in student orientation between the retiring director and myself was reflected in a student intake interview conducted in December, 1985. That month I was being mentored by the outgoing director in preparation to becoming the overall operational director of the school in January. In January, the outgoing director would become a member of the alternative school's board of directors.

The exiting director spoke in an authoritarian tone to the student, saying something like, "You only get one chance here or you're out! You must obey the rules here, or you're out! We are not going to put up with any behaviors that violate our rules! Do you understand?"

The student shook his head yes as the director motioned towards me, saying that I would be the new director of the school when the student started in January. He then asked me if there was anything I wanted to say to the new student.

As best I remember, I said, "Yes," and then said to the student, "Thank you for deciding to attend the alternative school and giving all of us a chance to show you that we care about you and we can really help you succeed. You are giving us this chance to prove to you how helpful this school can be. I know you won't regret your decision. Again, thank you."

It took about a year for the outgoing director to comment to me about that meeting. He said something like, 'When we had that interview in December with the new student, after what you said to him, I knew that you were the right person to replace me. I had become something I did not like. It was all the pressure I was under. You were right. I just wanted you to know that.'

Yes, I valued this man. He did many good things throughout his career and provided me with an excellent lesson about being the person in charge.

The implementation of strategies developed for this alternative school to assist its students caused the school to receive regional and national attention for its record of success. The book *A School for Healing: Alternative Strategies for Teaching At-Risk Students,* was written by Rosa L. Kennedy (the center's artist-in-residence) and me (the school's director). It was published by Peter Lang Publishing, NY, NY in 1999. It describes the program during my tenure there, January 1986 to August 1991. The book's jacket says the following: "*A School for Healing: Alternative Strategies for Teaching At-Risk Students* describes an alternative school that dealt with students who were expelled or suspended from public school and who perceived themselves as victims of injustice. It was assumed that they misinterpreted the facts of various situations or chose inappropriate strategies to correct real injustices. The task of the school was to help the students learn multiple perspectives for interpreting the actions of others and to teach them more appropriate ways of resolving injustices. Four students in the school relate their problems and describe, through a qualitative research interview process, how the school helped them. The book describes specific strategies the school used and concludes with suggestions to those who wish to establish a similar program."

Some of the strategies used by the school staff include the implementation of positive reinforcement through the creation of a school-wide token economic system, the engagement of the students in art activities, the use of community organizations, community volunteers (area artists, college and university students, faculty from departments such as English, law, counseling, physical education, human services), participatory management of the school by staff and students, and the overall avoidance of the use of punishment while recognizing the natural consequences of inappropriate behavior.

In 1990 the Southern Association of Colleges and Schools presented the program its Exemplary Dropout/Retention Program award. The school was also honored another year with the Best School/Best Principal Award in Knoxville. Nova University identified the alternative school as one of "Tomorrow's Innovations Today" in a publication. A university professor conducted significant evaluations of the program's positive effect on its students' lives and published those results. Several academic books reference the alternative school and its innovative strategies that produce successful outcomes. The school and its students received many other awards and recognitions. The school produced a school newspaper, a book of poetry, art contest winners and a weekly column written by the students in the local newspaper. The program was a success by most standards.

Interestingly, once the students gained control of their impulsive behaviors and were experiencing success in their lives, the alternative school was able to determine that approximately ten percent of the students qualified as intellectually gifted according to the state's education department standards of the time. The school's artist-in-residence reported that another fifteen percent or so of the students were considered to be artistically talented or gifted as judged by the quality of their art projects and awards that they received in regional, state or national art contests in which the artist-in-residence had the program engage.

My involvement in the program ended in August 1991. The official reason I was released was that the one school system still funding the program had been forced to close some schools because of integration issues. Principals from those schools were tenured in the school system. The school system could not continue contracting with an outside agency, LTVEC, for someone to be the principal of its alternative school while it was laying off tenured principals. I could understand that logic. However, the alternative school was technically under the control of a not-for-profit organization. It was true that without the funding from the only remaining school system, the alternative school would close. The fact that the school system considered the alternative school to be "its" school means that the school was a success. Remember, when I accepted the position as director of the school the goal was one of three things, one: it received new monies to keep operating; two, it was to be taken over by a school system and continue to function; or three, it would be so successful that others would know of its work and want to promote the strategies developed by the program.

Yes, the alternative school was kept alive by a school system, but many of the innovative strategies it used were not. Yes, over the years others have adopted many of the strategies used by our alternative school, the School for Healing. It has been reported that in school systems in the Alberta, Canada, area the *School for Healing* book is required reading for all new teachers. Some alternative schools in the state of Maine have reportedly been modeled after the alternative school. A search on Google has found that an academic book published in India makes extensive references (with footnotes) to the *School for Healing* book in support of its recommendations for improving schools in that country. Yes, the program was so successful that others know of its work and want to promote the strategies developed by the program.

Since many of the strategies used by the School for Healing were not continued under the leadership of the new director, the vast majority of the staff left the program within a couple of years in order to continue the strategies they had used at the school. One went to join an alternative school staff in Maine. Another began working in juvenile justice for another state. The ideas of the program continued to be spread. Most rewarding was the feedback from many staff members that former students had continued to communicate with them. All of the students who attended the alternative school were valued. That valuing was not misplaced.

The alternative school was technically under the control of a registered, non-profit organization's board of directors, and that organization had the authority to decide who its director would be. The reality was that the school system funding the school was the one in control. After the system assumed ownership of the school, a need arose to officially terminate the non-profit organization and to maintain relevant records. With the remaining funds in the non-profit's bank account, the organization contracted with the cooperative to handle the necessary details for official closure. High level administrators within the acquiring school system did have some criticism of the School for Healing.

An elected official from the immediate area decided to visit the alternative school. It had been reported that he said the school was a waste of money. It was true that the cost of serving a student at the alternative school was fifty percent higher than the cost of educating a student in the regular school program. When we met, I addressed his concerns by comparing the cost of assisting a student to be a productive citizen to the cost to society if the student continued to remain in conflict with much of society. The elected official ended the conversation stating that the school was a waste of money. What we needed to do was work with the poor young adults who were currently raising their babies. I replied that six of the school's students were currently raising their babies. He left without commenting.

On one occasion the alternative school refused to accept a student the public school system was referring to the school. After the alternative school's staff had interviewed the student in question, the staff concluded that the referred student needed much more extensive psychological interventions than it could provide. That situation provoked some criticism. Another criticism of the alternative school was that when a student's time of suspension was up, the student would be so happy to be returning to his regular school because "The student never wants to have to return to this alternative school," and that did not happen. More often than not, the students did not want to return to their regular schools. They wanted to remain at the alternative school. As one supervisor said to me, "That's just not right." When I heard those words, I thought to myself, "This culture's investment in punishment, in punishment often so harsh it becomes revenge, is very hard for many to let go of and to embrace healing strategies as the preferred way for assisting our troubled youth."

Writing grants for the University of Tennessee's College of Education and managing conferences for various departments allowed me to remain in contact with the school psychology training program. I attended meetings concerning that division and was on the committee that managed the newly revised doctoral internship program. The state board of healing arts had changed the requirements for licensure as a psychologist. Those changes reflected the new rules for accreditation adopted by the American Psychological Association, APA. Attending a school psychology APA accredited internship program was the gold standard of internship programs. Another accreditation that an internship program could obtain was slightly less rigorous but still a must for a school psychologist desiring to be licensed by the Board of Healing Arts. The least desired internship was a non-accredited one. The more rigorous the accreditation for an internship program, the better the employment opportunities for the intern would be.

In the early 1990's Steve McCallum, chairman, Educational Psychology Department, College of Education, University of Tennessee, completed the application for the second desired level of accreditation for the school psychology internship program. Both this level of accreditation and the APA's level required a doctoral-level school psychologist to supervise an intern and required that the intern be allowed to attend regularly scheduled individual and group supervision sessions. Many other time-consuming requirements existed.

All of those requirements meant that the full-time intern would not be available to be in a school much more than twenty hours a week. Most school systems were not employing doctoral-level school psychologists at that time which meant that they could not provide the required supervision from a doctoral-level school psychologist. Nor could most school systems provide the release time to the program for the required supervision of either the supervising school psychologist or the intern. However, many of the larger city school systems and generously funded school systems could afford to support an accredited internship program.

The University of Tennessee's internship program began providing school psychology doctoral internships through the cooperation of the Knox County School System and a large, non-profit organization that had a licensed doctoral school psychologist in its employment. Dr. Ron Carlini, a licensed school psychologist with Knox County Schools, was provided some release time to handle the re-accreditation process. The complications of that process increased, demanding more time of Dr. Carlini than he could provide. The university made an arrangement with the cooperative for me to invest the time necessary to renew the second level of accreditation and coordinate the entire internship program. Fortunately, the university was able to continue to reimburse Dr. Carlini for conducting the internship's group supervision sessions as required by the APA accreditation standards. The supervision sessions were held after schools had closed for the day. It was a privilege to work with Dr. Carlini over my fifteen years with the internship consortium.

My involvement in the accreditation process evolved to include completing the requirements of the internship program for APA accreditation. The cooperative became the fiscal agent of the internship program, which included processing its payroll and expense reimbursements. I was also able to be the one-on-one internship supervisor each year for a few interns that were assigned to LTVEC school systems. As training director and chief operating officer of the internship program, I was able to lead the program, the Tennessee Internship Consortium in Psychology (TIC), to be accredited by the American Psychological Association. I fulfilled my role in TIC from 1999 until my retirement in 2014. Of course, both LTVEC and I were reimbursed each year for our services.

A modest grant from the state brought about the creation of the cooperative's assistive technology program. The grant required that an occupational therapist be employed to provide direct assistance to children with special educational needs in acquiring and using assistive technological tools in the accomplishment of their IEP goals and objectives. Many of the cooperative's school systems did not have someone knowledgeable in this field to assist them in making appropriate decisions. They, like many other school systems, relied upon outside agencies and businesses to evaluate a child's needs for technological devices and then make their recommendations. The problem for the school systems was that many of those recommendations were for the most advanced device capable of meeting the child's needs once the child learned how to use the equipment. Unfortunately, these devices were often the most expensive ones.

A few months after the equipment had been purchased, it sat in a corner closet not being used. When the child first tried to use the equipment, the computerized controls were far more complicated than anything the child had ever used. The gap between what the child knew about computer-related controls and what the child had to know in order to operate the new assistive technology tool was too large to be overcome both for the child and the child's teachers. The end result was that the purchasing school system had a lot of expensive equipment in storage. No one in the system knew how to operate it. The agency recommending the state-of-the-art equipment wanted the best equipment for the child who needed it under the assumption that someone in the system would see to it that the child would quickly be taught how to use it. That assumption did not fit the realities.

The assistive technology equipment that was immediately needed for the special education child was something that was a reasonable step above the current competency level of the child. Once the new level of competency was obtained, the child would move up to the next level of equipment sophistication and on and on until the child had reached the level of technological proficiency that they could operate the state-of-the-art equipment originally recommended by other agencies.

The first two occupational therapists employed to provide this new service found the resistance from other agencies to be stressful. The agencies interpreted the recommendations to purchase less sophisticated equipment for the child to be an attempt by the schools to simply save money by not purchasing what the child needed. In turn, those agencies often shared their opinions with the parents of the disabled children and encouraged them to file for a due process hearing against the school system. To avoid that difficult process, many school systems simply agreed to buy the most technologically advanced equipment, knowing that in a few months efforts to use it would cease. Adding the therapists' stress was the resistance some special education staff displayed at having to spend their time trying to learn a technology they did not understand when they could be sharing one-on-one time with a child doing things that they knew how to do and that the child enjoyed.

Both of the occupational therapists in this new role decided that their best contributions in assisting children with disabilities was in the delivery of their occupational therapy skills. That led to the employment of the third occupational therapist to function as the head of this project. That occupational therapist, Janice Reese, was a perfect fit. She understood all of the issues and had the patience to work with the parents and school system staff to gain their support in making the necessary progressive steps in the use of assistive technology. As the children acquired the skills needed to operate more technologically advanced equipment, those devices would be available to them. That was the beginning of a program that grew into one of the largest programs the cooperative has at the time of this writing.

As the cooperative progressed over the years, it received grants from various agencies to deliver highly successful progressive intervention that changed people's lives but were not continued beyond the life of the grants. In turn, issues raised by the cooperative's staff caused changes to happen within the school systems that evolved into new programs for the cooperative to deliver.

For example, the cooperative's promotion of the "full-service schools" concept led to the cooperative's providing after-school and before-school programs for children.

The cooperative's staff's continual attempts to address the needs of the children with behavioral problems in the schools resulted in a program to provide the services of behavior analysts to schools. The cooperative's focus and corrective strategies in this area were a key component of the work it did in the alternative school. Serious behavioral issues of students remain a major problem for educators today. It may be an area for further growth within the cooperative's delivery of services model.

As early as 1973, the state had difficulty in addressing behavioral issues within its special education laws. Classroom behavior problems remain as one of the biggest concerns teachers have today. These facts speak to the need for this issue to be addressed. In 1973 one of the listed disabilities in the long list of disabilities that had to be addressed in the new law was something like, "Behavioral Problems." So many children fit this category that a more restrictive term evolved into "Serious Behavioral Problems," and then it became something like "Emotionally Disturbed," and then it changed into something like "Seriously Emotionally Disturbed." Of course, each new title accompanied complex definitions of those terms. The end result has been that special education funds have gotten progressively harder to obtain for children who have behavioral difficulties.

I think this is a continuing reflection of the culture of our times. If, on the first day of school, a first grade, six-year-old girl walks into a classroom, rushes to a back corner of the room, sits in that corner on the floor, puts her coat over her head and starts sobbing, we have the impulse to help her. She has a behavioral problem. We want to comfort her. Yet, if a boy enters his first-grade classroom on the first day of the year and starts pushing other children out of his way, shouts at the teacher, refuses to follow her direction and then starts to scream at everyone, we want to punish him. He clearly has a behavioral problem.

If the behavioral-problem person is pathetic in the display of their problem, we want to help that person, and if the behavioral problem person is aggressive, we want to punish that person. At some point we must provide healing assistance to those with behavioral problems regardless as to how those problems are displayed.

Another area for expanding the scope of services that past activities have brought to light through LTVEC is providing more appropriate service to the systems' gifted student population, particularly in our rural school systems. I'm reminded of a presentation I made years ago at an environmental education conference in Middle Tennessee. My topic was engaging gifted students in activities concerning the environment. In the presentation, I referred to the lack of resources to stimulate gifted children and to the little or no relevant understanding of massive differences in conceptualization between an average child and the child that is three standard deviations above that normal range of intelligence.

After my presentation, a teacher approached me to confirm what I had said. He stated that he was a history teacher in a rural high school. Because of a shortage of math and science teachers in the small system, he was also the math and science teacher. In addition, he was the high school's field and track coach and did some other special tasks. The knowledge of a student in his math class far exceeded his. The student had been in his math class last year and displayed very advanced abilities in math. The teacher relied on the student to answer math questions from the other students when he simply did not know the answers. At the start of the current year's math class, he told the gifted student that he did not have to do anything in math for the whole year because the teacher knew that the gifted student knew everything in the math book already. He did ask the student to assist him some when he couldn't get a math concept across to the rest of the class. The teacher confessed that he felt guilty about not being able to provide more to the student.

Sometime around the middle of the school year school the

teacher received a notice from the University of Tennessee about a science contest for high school students. He thought this might be of interest to his gifted student. He could work on it during the math class. He passed on the notice to the student. The notice contained the instructions required for submissions to the contest. The gifted student thanked him but never commented on it as weeks passed. One day the student gave the teacher a handwritten paper with all kinds of math equations on it and some kind of title that was about a proof for something about the theories of quantum mechanics and relativity. It was beyond the teacher's understanding, but he agreed to submit it to the contest officials at the university.

After the passage of time, he received a letter from the director of the university's science contest stating that the paper had been disqualified because the student had plagiarized someone else's work. The teacher knew that was impossible. He knew that the child's family did not have a book or a magazine in the house nor did the school possess a book that had this kind of math in it. A week or so later he received another letter from the director saying that on further investigation it had been determined that the child had not plagiarized someone else's work. The paper represented original research and was a breakthrough in research of its kind. The letter went on to state that the paper was still disqualified because by the time it was discovered that it was original work, the date for submission of projects to the contest had passed.

That was a disturbing story. In the cafeteria that evening, I was eating supper at a large round table that had all of its chairs occupied by conference attendees. I only knew one or two of them sitting at the table. I could not help myself; I shared the teacher's story to prove my point that we need to do more to serve our gifted children. When I had finished telling it all, the man sitting beside his wife identified himself as the director of the university's science contest and stated that I had misrepresented the facts of the situation. He went on to explain what he meant. There he was in his office, and he receives this handwritten notebook paper of pages of math equations that ends in some sort of proof. The instructions for submission of a science project to the contest clearly stated that the paper should be typed and references provided.

This student's paper did not have one reference. However, the director was troubled by the paper. It professed to be in an area of science that was not his expertise. He decided to ask some physicist colleagues of his to look at it and tell him what they thought. They came back all excited. This was a breakthrough research paper. It proved something that had never been proved before. Well, that was why the director sent the second letter acknowledging that the student had not plagiarized his work and acknowledging that it represented a scientific breakthrough. However, this discovery happened after the deadline for submission of projects to the contest, so the paper was still disqualified.

I thanked the director for bringing forth facts that I didn't know concerning the incident. In my mind, I thought that the director had once again proven my point. We as educators need to develop more effective ways of assisting our gifted students. Hopefully, the cooperative will be a future catalyst for addressing these needs.

FIFTEEN
EVOLUTIONS IN UNDERSTANDING AND BELIEFS

As noted earlier, one never stops learning about a culture whether it is the culture you live in, the culture you have moved to or the one you are visiting. So it was for me during my time with the cooperative. I constantly encountered outstanding educators who were committed individuals in assisting children, teachers and parents. There were others who were more focused on their personal goals or the goals of the group with which they identified. To find someone who considered their orientation might be incorrect was difficult. From their perspective, they were the "good guys." You and I share this tendency.

When I encountered someone promoting a position that was harmful to the goals of the cooperative, I had to fight the urge to consider that person as "not good." I had to work on valuing their interpretation of the situation even when disagreeing with it. Naturally, I would try to present my position in such a persuasive manner that my view would prevail. Regardless of the success of that, the person disagreeing with me was teaching me about their interpretation of the situation. That interpretation was shaped in large part by the culture of which that person was a part and by the passage of time. Allow me to provide you with some of the situations that presented themselves as examples of these issues.

The pressure of the lack of adequate funding for educational services has always been an issue for the cooperative and its school systems. The first supervisor of special education in a large, mountainous school system was simply outstanding. In order to save money, he carried many tools in the trunk of his car so that when a special education bus broke down, he could drive to it and repair the vehicle as it sat on the side of the road. This saved him from having to use funds from his budget for towing and repairs. Any money spent on those services reduced the funds he had to spend on meeting the needs of children. The demands on his professional time were massive. Meetings to attend, reports to write, records to maintain, and a host of other tasks to accomplish were included his role as the supervisor of the system's special education program. I admired him. He was a powerful force for good. Despite my admiration for him, we did have our moments of disagreement.

Two such incidents of disagreements stand out for me as I reflect on those first few years of the cooperative. One concerned the co-op's search for a speech therapist to work in the system. The most qualified applicant had just finished her master's degree and was fully credentialed. She was very articulate and pleasant with a developed sense of humor. There was no doubt that she was the most qualified applicant and would be an excellent therapist for the system's children. I was aware of a problem. The system's plan was to have the new speech therapist work in the schools located near the state boundary line. In that mountainous area there had been a shooting of two graduate students from the area's university. They were reported to be from India. Rumor had it that any people of color in that area at night would be shot. Apparently, the graduate students were sightseeing and had gotten lost driving the back roads. According to news reports, that night they were shot to death while driving their car. The speech therapist I was recommending to be employed by the cooperative to work in that area was a black woman.

I explained the situation to her. She was adamant that she wanted the position. She was not afraid.

I recommended her to the system's supervisor, this man I admired. After explaining that the speech therapist was a black woman, the supervisor said that we could not do that. Her life would be in danger. I pointed out that she would be in those schools during the day and never at dusk or later. It was still too dangerous, he thought. The road from the main city of the county to the mountain schools was a narrow, two-lane with no businesses or houses on it for long stretches. Someone might just decide to run her off the road because she was black. The supervisor requested that I explain the danger she faced if she worked there while he spoke to the superintendent about the situation.

I explained to the applicant how dangerous the system thought it would be for her to accept a position there. The speech therapist was adamant that she wanted the position. She was not afraid. She did not believe that anything would happen to her.

Once again, I relayed the information that this applicant, this most qualified of all the applicants, wanted the position. The supervisor asked me to not employ her because it was so dangerous for her. She could not be protected on those isolated roads. I stated that I was required by law to offer the position to the most qualified person. She was the most qualified applicant. That was simply how it was. He said that he would speak to the superintendent again.

Later that day, I got a phone call from my friend, the supervisor, he told me that the school system was withdrawing its request for the co-op to hire a speech therapist on behalf of the system. I was saddened, but I understood the system's position even though I disagreed with it. It was painful explaining that the school system had withdrawn the funding to the cooperative to employ a speech therapist. We no longer had a position to offer her.

If it had been my decision, we would have employed the woman. A year or so after this unfolded, a really bad racial incident happened that caused me to realize that the school system was correct. The speech therapist's life would have been in great danger. She was at high risk of being seriously injured or killed. I have been asked not to describe the racial incident for fear that it would cause the general public to think everyone in that county was like the few racists living there. That terrible incident was stopped by the many outstanding citizens who intervened in that situation. In honor of those many kind and generous citizens, the vast majority of the citizens living in that area, I will not relate the event that caused me to be more sympathetic to the system's actions in its desire to protect a wonderful person who happened to be black.

In another incident that involved a conflict with the desires of a grandparent for his grandchild and the position of a school system in support of the findings of its school psychologist, I encountered a learning situation. The grandchild had been referred for an individual intelligence evaluation to determine if the child qualified as being gifted as defined by the state's department of education. The test results found the child to be quite intelligent but not gifted. The grandparent requested a meeting with the superintendent to challenge the school psychologist's evaluation results. I attended that meeting as did the system's supervisor of special education. The test results were clear. The child was definitely above average intellectually but was not gifted as giftedness was defined at that time.

Before the meeting, I was informed that the grandparent was a very well-respected professional who had provided valued professional services in that community for many years. He was an influencer of public opinion. In the meeting, this individual conducted himself as someone of major influence that the superintendent had better not cross. At one point in the meeting, he told the superintendent that he would see to it that the superintendent lost the next election if he did not have the system declare that his grandchild was gifted. After that threat, the grandfather left the meeting displaying great anger.

A few weeks later, I learned that the system was considering establishing its own definition of giftedness. That definition was far more liberal than the State Department's definition. I advised the system that it would cause the system a lot of difficulties in the future if it made this decision. The decision was opening the door to any parent that wanted the prestige of calling their child gifted. They could have half of all the children in the system identified as gifted and be faced with demands to have those children provided with special "gifted" programs. The system did not take my advice.

About fifteen or so years after the system created its own definition of giftedness and after the cooperative had ceased providing school psychological services to it, I happened to be passing by the office space for two of the system's school psychologists who were in deep consultation with each other. When they saw me, one of them addressed me angrily saying something like, "Jerry, you really created a mess when you changed the system's definition of giftedness." I responded in surprise, "Your system did that. I told the supervisor that this would happen. I begged him not to do it." They looked at me in surprise as I walked away.

Another example of a powerful member of a community disagreeing with one of the cooperative's psychological reports contains some interesting insights concerning the valuing of professionals within our schools. A graduate assistant had completed his assessment of a referred student. He had recorded some unusual issues with the standard testing results which caused him to administer another set of tests that focused on the specific issues the other tests raised. Those tests confirmed what he had suspected were the underlying issues that had caused the child to be referred in the first place. Just to be certain of the accuracy of his conclusions, he conferred with his professors at the university and with me.

We agreed with the graduate assistant's conclusions concerning the student's underlying problem. The student had a rare disorder that would cause the student's muscular control to progressively deteriorate. Research in the area indicated that with targeted therapeutic interventions, that deterioration could be significantly reduced. The graduate assistant's report was submitted to the school system and the parent. The child's father, an elected officeholder in the region, was outraged by the report. He insisted that nothing was wrong with his child. He wanted me to be fired for allowing my graduate assistant to write such an untruth in a report. The incompetence of the cooperative for employing someone like me who let a college trainee write such falsehoods about his child was proof that the school system should immediately cut all ties with the cooperative and the cooperative should fire me, the licensed psychologist who didn't know what he was doing.

I met with the psychology intern to explain the parent's concern and his demands. We reviewed the data that had led to the diagnosis in the report. The intern's diagnosis was correct. He was not to worry over the father's challenge. The cooperative and the professional community would support him and his report. I reassured the school system that the tests were administered correctly and that the results clearly supported the conclusions in the psychological report. The system's representatives said they would keep me informed of further developments in this situation. The next communication from the system to me was that the father was sending the child to a national center, several states away, that had specialized knowledge concerning the condition his child was incorrectly reported to have. Once that center had proven how incompetent the cooperative was, he would see to it that the cooperative, the intern and I were punished.

Several weeks passed with no further feedback coming from the school system about the results of the national center's evaluation of the child. Finally, a supervisor in the school system told me that the national center had sent them a copy of their report. The report contained their interpretation of the testing they had performed, their conclusions of the child's condition and an analysis of the intern's psychological report. The national center's report stated that they completely agreed with the conclusions of the intern's report. In the national center's report was praise for the excellence of the intern's report and with the intern's conclusions. In agreement with the intern, they recommended that early therapeutic interventions for the child now would make it highly likely that the seriousness of the child's condition would be reduced as the child entered adulthood. The school system indicated that the father insisted that there was nothing wrong with his child as he refused to allow his child to receive physical and occupational therapy along with other services the system wanted to provide the child.

Several months later it was reported that the child had been removed from the school system's rolls. The school system did not mention this situation to me again. Sometime later, I learned from news reports that the father had been removed from his elected position as a result of issues not related to his negative concerns about the cooperative. As a doctoral level psychologist, this intern went on to become a nationally recognized researcher/provider in addressing adolescent issues.

Being confronted with the struggles encountered when trying to facilitate change within regional or national organizations operating on larger platforms than those of local school systems provided me with insights into the role the educational cooperative was fulfilling. Here are a few examples of those learning situations.

The director of the Loudon County/Lenoir City Vocational Center, Coy Gibson, was an outstanding innovator. He was constantly coming up with news ways of training students to obtain trade skills that would provide them with rewarding employment opportunities after their graduation. Coy was an asset to the entire community in his ability to analyze the training needs a corporation or large business would have for its workforce if they decided to build a factory in the region. That knowledge made him an excellent recruiter for the region's chambers of commerce. What a privilege it was for the cooperative to be able to relocate to the vocational center when it had to leave the Blount County area! Coy and his staff were very supportive of the cooperative's activities. It was simply a pleasure to exchange ideas with Coy about so many educational issues. He was a person with extraordinary insights.

One idea he presented during our informal discussions was the need for a pre-employment training center that industries could use while they were building a factory. The pre-employment center could address a long-standing problem that new industries encountered when building a factory. The typical downtime for a business from the time the decision was made to build a factory to having the factory produce a product represented lost revenue. Strategies that reduced the timespan from the start of the building to production would produce significant savings to the business. Any region in the country that had a way of significantly reducing the downtime to production would have a major edge in recruiting business to its location.

As Coy explained it, the typical build-to-production cycle entails first buying the land and building the building. Once the building is built, the heavy manufacturing equipment needed to produce the product must be bought, shipped, and installed. Then a workforce must be trained to operate the production machinery. Not until the factory building is built can the business obtain the machinery needed for production. Logic would have the machinery purchased while the building was under construction, but that can't happen, for the business has no place to store all the equipment going into the new factory. So the downtime is having to wait until the factory building is built, and the equipment is shipped to the building site and installed. Once the equipment is ready to operate, time has to be spent to train the workforce in how to operate the heavy equipment. Once the workforce is trained, production can start.

Coy's solution to the problem was to have a pre-employment training center built that could serve the immediate region. The pre-employment center would have solid, reinforced floors strong enough to hold heavy manufacturing equipment with equally heavy electrical wiring to power the equipment. The building would have wide loading docks to unload the equipment from trucks and then the transportation system needed to move the equipment into the building for easy installation. If the equipment needed by the business arrived in the area near where the manufacturing building was being built, the time it took to get the equipment installed in the new building would be cut, thereby reducing the amount of downtime the business had before actual production would begin.

Further reducing downtime, once the heavy equipment was installed in the pre-employment building, the area vocational schools could start training the workers for the factory in the use of the equipment. Thus, the workers were being trained while the building was being built. As soon as the building was ready, the equipment would immediately be installed, and the workforce would immediately start production. The saved time from concept to productivity for a business would be greatly reduced through the use of the pre-employment training center. The savings in starting a new factory near an existing pre-employment training center would be a contributing factor for any business in deciding to build a factory in East Tennessee as contrasted to starting a factory in some other state.

I thought Coy's concept was outstanding and encouraged him to write a proposal and submit it to the state. He said that he would submit it if I would write the proposal. I agreed. With the written proposal, we became a team in presenting it to funding sources. Coy contacted the vocational school directors in Blount and Monroe Counties and obtained their written support of the project. I was able to obtain the free services of a large architectural firm to draw the plans for a pre-employment training center that met our specifications. The drawings of the center were impressive.

Coy and I met with the Tennessee Valley Authority (TVA) business development department. I think one of TVA's vice presidents and his immediate deputy met with us. Before the meeting, I had sent them the introductory summary of the pre-employment center proposal. The deputy to the vice president was not supportive of the proposal. The vice president said that he would study the full proposal, consult with others in TVA and get back with us as to what support TVA could provide the project.

Next, Coy and I went to Nashville to ask the state's Commissioner for Business Development for his department's support. Again, I had sent him the introduction and summary paper explaining the project's overall proposal. The commissioner was most cordial to us. He said that he liked the concept and had researched the concept to see if any other states had a similar project. None of them did. This was an original idea. It was a real innovation. He thought it could work. However, Tennessee was a poor state. It did not have the revenue to risk on an untried project. He expressed his regrets that he could not support our efforts.

Our second meeting with TVA was just with the vice president's deputy. He informed us that TVA did not think the project was feasible. It just would not be effective in attracting business to the region. There it was. We were unable to obtain funds for the project.

A few months later, Coy invited me to be his guest at a large meeting TVA was conducting. He said that he thought that it would be important for me to attend. He did not explain what the meeting was about. If he thought it was important for me to attend, then it was.

The TVA auditorium was much larger than I had anticipated. Several hundred people must have been in attendance. Coy and I sat in the balcony section. I did not know why so many people were there. An official of TVA called the meeting to order. He said he was pleased to announce that with funding from TVA and the Tennessee Business Development Department, a Pre-Employment Training Center would be created near Johnson City. Then he called the newly appointed director of the Pre-Employment Training Center to the podium to explain the center and its functions. After a round of applause, the new director began explaining the activities of the center. He got a little confused in what he was describing. He said that the best way of explaining the pre-employment training center was to read the introduction from the original grant proposal. Placing pages of paper on the podium's flat surface, he read the multipage introduction. It was word for word what I had written and presented to TVA and the Tennessee Business Development Department. I was stunned.

As Coy and I were leaving the TVA auditorium with the crowd of attendees, Coy said, "You're a very good writer, Jerry." That was the only comment made about the announcement. I don't know if that center was a success or not. A few years later I read in the newspaper that TVA was funding a pre-employment training center near Tellico Plains in Monroe County. The new director was a former TVA administrator. He was the individual at TVA that told Coy and me that the pre-employment training center would never work. As far as I could tell, the Tellico Plains center never brought new industry into the region.

I admit to thinking that the cooperative should have had the support of those agencies. We would have done an excellent job of fulfilling their vision. Then I would reflect that the goal of the cooperative is to bring in new ideas that will help people and their children. We did that by introducing the ideas contained within the pre-employment training center. We performed a good service to the region by proposing a plan that might one day lead to success. We fulfilled our mission once again.

Another major proposal that was developed through the cooperative but not implemented was the development of an enrichment opportunity for the area's gifted students. The project began with a friendly conversation between a scientist working at the Oak Ridge National Laboratory and me. I was sharing my concerns for the intellectually highly gifted population in the region's high schools. My experiences with this population had caused me to consider this population as the most underserved of all the subgroups in the public schools. In the main, so many of these students are simply bored. My scientist friend commented that the Oak Ridge National Laboratory had tried to help in this area but had basically failed. They do have a program that pairs gifted high school and college students with scientists at the lab, but the students don't stay long. All the gifted students end up doing are cleanup tasks, washing out test tubes and things like that. The researchers don't have time to talk to the students to teach them enough to do something worthwhile. In the main, the students just start not showing up.

I said that these very bright students want to get involved in state-of-the-art research. They want to understand what the issues are when doing that kind of research. They need to be able to interact with the researchers on a personal basis. My friend asked how we could cause that to happen. I noted that at the time, TVA had sitting vacant near Vonore, Tennessee, a state-of-the-art environmental testing station that was even capable of testing for radiation in the atmosphere. Well, it wasn't totally vacant, I noted. A paper box company was reported to be storing some of their boxes in it. The testing station was built as part of the TVA model city project but ended up not being used when TVA decided to not go ahead with that project. We could use that facility to have the high school students do real scientific work beside those engaged in meaningful science projects, but I don't know how we could fund it or where we would find first-rate researchers to volunteer to work with the students. If we could get a project like that going as a summer program, we would need nearby housing for the students. Maybe some colleges, like Maryville College, could make some dorms available during the summer. With the co-op's offices located in Loudon we were about halfway between Vonore and Maryville. It was perfectly located to be able to manage the gifted project if it ever developed as hoped.

We decided to pursue these ideas and see what just might be possible. I would check with Maryville College about dorm space, with TVA about the use of the environmental testing station, and the University of Tennessee about funding. My friend said that he would talk to some of his scientific researcher friends about volunteering for such a project and see what funding sources he could find.

Well, Maryville College was definitely interested in providing dorm space for such a project. I spoke with the overall dean of scientific activities on the campus of the University of Tennessee about possibly supporting and funding such a project. He said that it was an interesting concept. He would need time to think about it. I felt certain the cooperative's board of directors would support the project and allow the cooperative to serve as coordinator of the project. The TVA vice president for community affairs and I had briefly interacted with each other during the first few years I was with the co-op. I spoke with him concerning the environmental lab at Vonore. He wanted me to write a proposal for using the facility that included as many details of the gifted project as I could, so that he could present it to the chairman's staff for their consideration.

While I was doing all of that, my scientist/researcher friend had obtained a commitment from the director of the Sandia National Laboratories and the head of Corning Glass's Ceramics Research Division to engage in state-of-the-art research projects with the selected gifted students. He had also obtained an appointment for me to discuss funding of the project with the acting director of the National Science Foundation in Washington, D. C. I shared this information with the cooperative's board of directors. They agreed to pay for my expenses to and from Washington.

The morning interview the director of the National Science Foundation went beyond my expectations. After entering his office and being offered a chair beside his desk, I noticed that his tie tack was a little oversized eagle. It looked a lot like the eagle insignia of an Army colonel. He began our conversation by saying that he would not be meeting with me if they had not checked me out. He then began to praise a project I had been involved with at the Special Warfare Center. He described my actions in great detail. I had never spoken of that project to anyone. Something was going on about my being there that was beyond my understanding. He went on to say that my work at the cooperative had been admired by a lot of people. There was no question, he said, about my ability to successfully develop my gifted center project. My problem was that I did not have the support of the local people in the area. Without that support, the community resistance would be too great to overcome. However, he was willing to make a pledge to me. If I could raise ten thousand dollars for the project from local individuals in the area, he would see to it that I got all the money I needed to fully fund the project, on one condition. I could not tell anyone about our bargain. In the back of my mind, like him, I seriously doubted that I could raise that kind of money.

The director graciously took me to a high-end restaurant and insisted on treating me to lunch. Among other items, he ordered a martini while offering me one. I passed on the offer. We shook hands as we parted, and he wished me good luck.

I knew that I could not raise significant funds for the project by walking into a business and asking for a donation. I would be perceived as a totally unknown stranger who was panhandling. I would need someone connected with the school systems who was valued by the business owners and who valued me to be with me in requesting a donation for this project. I shared with local school officials I thought would help me, that if I could raise ten thousand dollars or so from their communities to launch the gifted project, I was pretty sure we could get the rest of the funds we needed from other funding sources. I explained the project in detail and the support that was pledged to it at that time.

No money was raised for the project. Several months later I read in the newspaper that the University of Tennessee science departments had entered into a special partnership with Oak Ridge National Laboratories to begin a project for gifted public school and college students to be mentored in actual research projects by the scientists at Oak Ridge.

I spoke with my scientist/research friend about what I had read and asked if he knew anything about it. He did not. It was a surprise to him.

Not too long after that, TVA informed me that the director, David Freeman, made the decision not to allow the Vonore research building to be used for our gifted project. He said that that environmental research building had been paid for from electric user fees and therefore should be sold to generate money for the benefit of the rate payers.

About twenty years after we worked on this project, I had the opportunity to ask a retired senior supervisor from one of the co-op's member systems located near Vonore if he remembered that gifted project I was working on to use the Vonore Environmental Research Building for state-of-the-art research activities for the area's gifted students. He did remember it. I explained to him the offer made to me to fund the project if I could raise ten thousand dollars from the community. The bargain was only good if I would not tell anyone about it. I reminded him that I had asked him and others for help in raising these funds. Yes, the supervisor remembered my trying to raise money for the project. Well, I asked, why didn't anyone help? His reply was that they thought I was lying. No one believed me. They did not think anyone that important, any of those scientists that important, would ever be interested in doing all that for a little rural area like theirs. He said that he did believe me now. He didn't think I had the proof that those nationally prominent figures were actually going to do what I claimed. He was sorry that they were wrong.

Once again, I avoided being angry by thinking that the ideas for enhancing the educational experiences of the area's gifted high school students we developed did become a reality. That was the important truth. The cooperative was successful in promoting a strategy for helping our gifted youth, in providing them with a richer educational environment. At the end of the day, that is what all our efforts are about.

SIXTEEN
THE COOPERATIVE IS A TOOL

The educational cooperative has been and continues to be a tool for educators to obtain services that remove blocking barriers in assisting children. This tool is a remarkable one as it continually develops new approaches to be of assistance within the constantly evolving realities it confronts in long-held belief systems, changing focuses of government, and personalities concerned with issues not related to meeting the needs of children.

When I started with LTVEC in 1973, I was told that there were approximately seventy-five educational cooperatives in the state. To the best of my knowledge, the Tennessee Educational Cooperative, which is the logical continuation of LTVEC, is now the only functioning educational cooperative in the state. What happened to all the others? I only knew of four other cooperatives, and what I knew was minimal. Due to funding issues, one of them evolved into becoming the fiscal agent for the HeadStart program in its region. Another one seemed to serve as a political launching platform for its director. It was rumored that funds from one school system were sometimes used in other school systems. This practice hastened the closure of that co-op.

The longest-lasting one I know of was supported by East Tennessee State University as part of its community outreach program. I was told by the director of that cooperative that the university provided the cooperative with free office space and fifty thousand dollars a year for administrative expenses. When the university's support ended, so did the cooperative. A rumor about a more distant cooperative's demise was that the largest member school system dominated the smaller systems to the extent that the largest system's superintendent caused his wife to be the director of one of the cooperative's programs despite her lack of qualifications for the position. Regardless of the truth of those rumors, it was said that disagreements between what the largest system wanted and what the smaller systems wanted brought about the end of that one. The western part of the state seemed to have a large number of educational cooperatives. I knew nothing about them.

Perhaps a hint of a common problem within many cooperatives of that time lies in the fact that somewhere in the late 1970's or the 1980s, the state passed legislation requiring educational cooperatives to present annual reports to the Department of Education documenting the administrative charge attached to a program that delivered direct services to children. The legislation wanted to know what percentage of a dollar provided for direct service to a child went to cover the administrative costs of the cooperative so that that sum could be compared to those charged by individual school systems and private providers.

LTVEC had those kinds of records readily available, but it would take a little time to translate them into whatever format the state would want. As the date for the first annual report required by the new legislation approached, LTVEC had not received any information concerning the filing of the mandated administrative charges report. At a statewide conference, I had an opportunity to speak with the state's commissioner of education about the filing. I noted that LTVEC had the correct information but needed guidance to know the format the state wanted the co-op to use in the report.

The commissioner told me to forget about it. The Department of Education would never ask for it. During my time with the cooperative, we never received such a request.

Several grants that the co-op received during my tenure with the cooperative were not renewed. That does not mean that they failed, far from it. To the best of my knowledge all of our results met and exceeded the grants' objectives. One grant that comes to mind that demonstrates this point was designed to improve the educational level of poor women with dependent children who were receiving financial aid. Their academic levels were so low that there was little hope they could find meaningful employment. On one standardized test, they scored around first-grade levels in math and reading. The cooperative's mission was to raise their test scores high enough that job counselors could reasonably expect to assist them in finding work. The funding source assumed that having them attend classes as if they were in school would cause the women to do better academically.

The women dramatically improved after two years in LTVEC's program. The improvement took place for reasons other than receiving academic instruction. They did attend classes set up just for them that coached them in reading and math skills. During those hours together in the "classroom," the women would share their life troubles with the instructor. The problems they were having had a constant theme. The choices they made to solve those problems were flawed. The classroom instructor held a Ph. D. in psychology. She would explore with the women various options they could apply to their decision-making processes that would enhance their skills in finding more successful solutions to difficulties they were facing.

As their decisions began producing better results for them, their self-concepts began to improve. As a result, their confidence in being able to be successful in learning improved. It took about a year for them to really believe that they could learn to read, solve math problems and accomplish life goals. Once they reached that emotional level, the question was not if they could learn to read. The question was, would they get enough sleep, because they wanted to stay up all night practicing reading. They knew they could succeed. They were going to study as hard as they could because they knew they could do it. No one or no life situation was going to hold them back. Within a few years, some participants had written books that were to be published.

Funding for this project was renewed several times. Instructors changed, but the focus of the interaction with the following groups of women remained the same as did the results. The program funding agency discontinued the grants due to the government's change in focus for assisting these people. While the co-op could not continue the program, the effects of it went on for generations. The lives of the women changed dramatically for the good as did the lives of their children and grandchildren.

Once we as individuals experience dramatic changes for the good, we do not want to go back to the old, ineffectual ways. The behavior of the alternative school staff demonstrated that. They were teaching in a negative, punitive environment when the cooperative's positive program strategies were introduced to them in the middle of the school year. They had to dramatically change the way they interacted with the students. They had to be positive and supportive of the students' efforts rather than punitive and rushing to turn the page of a textbook. They did it, and they did it well. When circumstances dramatically changed and they were confronted with going back to some of the old ways, they resigned. They could not return to the old ways.

The values reflected in the functioning of the cooperative and reflected in the strategies implemented at the alternative school do not need a grant to cause them to be realized. The cooperative had a woman on welfare assigned for mentoring to the co-op's accountant/office manager, Billie Kate, as part of a state program placing such individuals in mentored employment situations. We saw behavior changes take place. The woman met the stereotypical image of a young, black, unmarried female with a small child. This person was so appreciative for the opportunity to be working with the cooperative. She was eager to learn and desired to be of true value to the office manager and the cooperative staff. Her work truly enhanced the appearance and function of the cooperative's office activities. One morning she called in to report that her child was sick, and she was taking him to the emergency room. The next morning, she was on time to the office. Billie Kate and the rest of us were concerned for her and her child. In our world, having to take your child to the emergency room meant a crisis was at hand. The young woman reported that her child had a simple cold. That's why she took him to the emergency room.

The office manager told her that she should have taken the child to their local physician. It would have been far less expensive. The young woman disagreed. It would have cost the same. Besides, since she was on welfare, the state paid the emergency fee. The office manager pointed out that it was taxpayers who were paying the extra money it cost to go to the emergency room. Did the young woman want anyone to pay for her child's medical bills at a higher cost than it needed to be? This young mother simply did not think it was more expensive to get services at the emergency room rather than at a local doctor's office. If that was truly the case, of course, she said, she would go to the doctor's office with her child. The office manager proposed to take the woman to the accounting office of the emergency room to establish how much it cost for a visit there to treat a child's cold and then to go to a local doctor's office and see what the charges would be. When they returned from the trip, the young woman expressed regret at causing the extra medical expenses. Her family became patients of a local physician. She explained that she just didn't understand and thanked everyone for helping her know the truth. Over and over the cooperative's work revolves around promoting understanding as contrasted to punishment for lack of understanding.

It is understandable that people in our culture do not always trust the motivation of organizations in general. It is understandable that some people in our culture think others lie often, and it is understandable that others want the control of those who can change their environment, and it is understandable that some educators do not understand that the professionals they work with must maintain their professional standards or they are not professionals. This does not mean that people should be punished for their lack of understanding. It means that people must be informed and that organizations have to demonstrate their trustworthiness. It means that professionals always have to speak the truth. It means that common goals can be supported by independent individuals, and it means that professionals are consistent in their professional behavior.

Because the cooperative has consistently demonstrated these positive characteristics over time, it has been successful. It has often taken the passage of time to show that what appeared to be failure in the moment proved to be a success. A few examples of this phenomenon follow.

Some years after Blount County Schools was no longer a member of the cooperative, on a Saturday morning I was walking across a large parking lot when I heard my name called out. An elementary school principal from Blount County Schools with whom I had had some significant disagreements was running up to me waving his hands. As he approached me, he said something like, 'I finally understood what you were telling me. I want to thank you so much. You helped me see things differently. Thank you!' I was stunned. I remember that we had had a conflict but did not remember what the conflict was and what school he was principal of. I just knew that my time with him had been successful when I had assumed that I had failed.

The school psychology graduate assistants did not want to go into one elementary school because the principal was so harsh and punitive to his students. I spoke to him about being more positive. That angered him. Some years later, a student entered his office and pointed a pistol at the principal, telling him that he was going to kill him. The principal spoke kindly to the child. He found ways of telling the child how much he valued the young person. His supportive nature was such that the child handed the pistol over to the man. After the incident was no longer newsworthy, this principal presented at many conferences about the importance of being kind and supportive of children. Maybe, just maybe, the graduate students and my planting the idea of being supportive rather than punitive to children played a role in how this man became an advocate for understanding and kindness as the way to improve student behavior. If my speculations are correct, it's certainly all right not to get the credit for this change. The changed behavior is the important outcome. In the end, it is all that matters.

Now, a twist on finding the good in a negative situation. I was asked to make a presentation to all of the administrators of a relatively large school system that the cooperative had once served. The request was that I speak about the strategies the alternative school used to produce the documented changes in the students who had all been expelled from regular school for seriously inappropriate behavior. When I arrived for the presentation, the new superintendent of the school system and key staff members were sitting in the center of the room with the other attendees sitting in chairs encircling them. I was to make my presentation in the center of the circle—well, almost at the center as that was where the superintendent and his senior staff were. I had a vague memory of having been in the school when the superintendent had served as a principal. That memory carried some lingering unease.

I began my presentation by describing the strategies we used in the alternative school and the success they produced. As I did, the superintendent would grunt, stretch out his legs, twist and turn as he shook his head. When I started citing the results of the research done to validate the program's successes the superintendent made loud groaning sounds. Looking straight at him and using his name, I asked him what was wrong. He seemed to be having a problem with what I was saying. His reply went like this, "You are lying! We all know the kind of kids you were dealing with. They're never going to change."

I interrupted him saying, "This was research done by independent parties. It is true."

"YOU ARE LYING!"

I turned from him and, with a little less enthusiasm, continued with my presentation.

Today, I reflect on that encounter. The person who invited me to make that presentation had to have known that the superintendent would be in attendance and would be hostile to what I was going to present. It took great courage for that staff person to invite me to the presentation. She had to have had support from other administrators in the school system to bring me forth knowing that my words would be antithetical to the beliefs of the new superintendent. My presentation was a tool to let the superintendent know that many of his administrators were not supportive of his negative approach to them and the way they served the children in that system. I was the tool they were using to stand up for positive support of their children. With that interpretation, my presentation was a success.

As my years with the cooperative passed and as superintendents, supervisors of special education and principals changed in every school system, I found that I often had to start all over in explaining the special education laws, the services provided through the cooperative, the cost benefits of those services, the guarantees to the system that their funds would not be used to pay for services to children in other systems and the reasons that the administrative costs are necessary and are a bargain. The educators with whom we had gone through all of this and who had understood the cooperative's value for their system were no longer there. We had to start over.

Finally, I came to better understand this re-education task. Let me explain it this way. If I'm a fifth-grade schoolteacher receiving a new group of fifth graders at the start of the school year, I greet them with joy. We progress through the school year, and they all have learned the fifth-grade material. I am pleased with our success. They go on to the sixth grade. Now it's the start of the next school year.

The new fifth-grade students enter the class. They do not know what last year's fifth graders learned. Should I be angry at them for not knowing what last year's fifth graders learned when they were ready to move on to the next grade? Of course not. I am pleased to once again be able to have the opportunity of sharing valuable information with my new students so they will be able to use it in the betterment of their lives and the lives of those they meet. Such is the case for the cooperative.

My years with LTVEC were constantly challenged with the uncertainty of knowing if it would be able to survive into the next year. It has survived and expanded its delivery of services model into so many school systems today that it is now known as the TENNESSEE EDUCATIONAL COOPERATIVE! The range of professional services it provides is so extensive that they need to be examined on TEC's website www.tn-edu.org in order to be fully appreciated.

I am so pleased to have had the opportunity through my years at the cooperative to work with so many talented educators, dedicated members of the TEC (LTVEC) Board of Directors and with so many professional service providers. My memories are bursting with stories to share with you about the many wonderful things the cooperative's staff has accomplished in helping our area's educators serve their students in a manner that makes us all proud! I thank you all!

AUTHOR NOTES

Some of the interactions described in this book have been shared in my podcast, "Finding My Way," as well as in another book I've written or in both a podcast and one of my books. The podcast can be accessed at findingmyway.libsyn.com. Rosa Kennedy and I wrote *A School for Healing: Alternative Strategies for Teaching At-Risk Students.* It was published in 1999 by Peter Lang Publishing, Inc, New York. Rosa was the artist-in-residence at the alternative school during my time there as the director. She inspired many of the students through engaging them in various art projects. She became so committed to the use of art instruction to assist children in expressing themselves that she obtained a doctorate in education. The first section of the book *A School for Healing: Alternative Strategies for Teaching At-Risk Students* is from her qualitative dissertation, which received the 1995 Educational Research Award for Best Dissertation in qualitative research from the American Educational Research Association.

Texas A & M University Press published *Reluctant Lieutenant: From Basic to OCS in the Sixties* in 2004. All of the chapters in *Reluctant Lieutenant* have been included in my podcasts. This book provides insights into the training model used by the Army during the Vietnam period. From past memories, I describe my personal experiences during eight weeks of basic training, eight weeks of advanced infantry training and six months of Infantry Officer Candidate School. The training strategies used by the Army at that time did not always teach the lessons the Army had intended to teach. I do not make reference to those strategies within this book, although I do reference some insights I gained in my two years at the Army's Special Warfare Center.

In 2022, Tree Shadow Press of New Wilmington, Pennsylvania, published *Finding My Way: A Memoir*. Many of the chapters in *Finding My Way: A Memoir* are included in the podcasts and some of those accounts are also in *Swimming Upstream: The Little Tennessee Valley Educational Cooperative*. I was pleased with the sixty-second trailer developed to promote the book, *Finding My Way*. You can access that trailer at https://youtu.be/NSnZy-Usc20.

The large number of graduate assistants, doctoral interns and professional school psychologists with whom I have had the honor of working with along with the many other professional service providers is beyond the scope of this book to recognize for their superior skills and dedication to assisting our children. As the years have passed and these gifted individuals developed their careers into award-winning honors, I thank them for being my teachers. Collectively, we have all learned so much about how to assist those in need and those beginning their professional careers. That knowledge will not be lost.

~ Jerry Morton

ABOUT THE AUTHOR

Because his Coast Guard family lived in eight different states as he was growing up, Jerry Morton attended multiple public schools. Starting life in Duluth, Minnesota, passing through the Midwest and down to the Texas gulf coast, Jerry experienced the diverse norms of various subcultures. He learned that despite appearances, we are all the same, united in our common humanity.

This awareness was enhanced in his pursuit of a master's degree in school psychology, then by his three years in the Army, and yet again by his two years as a school psychologist serving inner-city schools being integrated for the first time. After obtaining his Ph.D. in school psychology, he began his career leading an educational cooperative as it assisted multiple school systems to begin serving children with disabilities.

Through these varied life experiences, Jerry became aware of the stress that change can create within individuals and institutions. In turn, he learned many helpful strategies to use in assisting individuals and institutions confronted with change. Jerry and the staff of the cooperative implemented those strategies as they assisted school systems to develop educational services for their children with special needs.

www.ingramcontent.com/pod-product-compliance
Lightning Source LLC
LaVergne TN
LVHW100524110826
845146LV00002B/768